The Backward Glance: CS Lewis and Ireland

For Catherine

The Backward Glance:
CS Lewis and Ireland

Ronald W Bresland

The Institute of Irish Studies
The Queen's University of Belfast

First published in 1999
The Institute of Irish Studies
The Queen's University of Belfast

This book has received support from the Cultural Diversity Programme of the Community Relations Council, which aims to encourage acceptance and understanding of cultural diversity. The views expressed do not necessarily reflect those of the NI Community Relations Council.

British Library Cataloguing-In-Publication Data.
A catalogue record for this book is available from the British Library.

ISBN 0 85389 746 8

Set in Times
Printed by W. & G. Baird Ltd, Antrim

Contents

Acknowledgements

This book has grown out of my research during 1997–98 for the CS Lewis Centenary Group and I wish to thank those members who offered support and encouragement during this time. In particular a special word of thanks is due to Mr Tony Wilson for assistance with photographs for this work and who took me on a memorable and inspiring hike to the 'Shepherd's Hut'.

Special thanks are due to: Dr John Gillespie of the University of Ulster who read the work in progress and offered thoughtful and constructive criticism; Anthony Smith, President of Magdalen College, Oxford, for his generous hospitality and assistance; the staff of the Bodleian Library, Oxford, in particular Colin Harris for his courteous help with my many queries; Walter Hooper for his kindness and help and for making material available to me; the staff of the Marion E Wade Centre, Wheaton College, Illinois, in particular Chris Mitchell and Marjorie Mead who dealt with my countless queries; Rachel Churchill of CS Lewis Pte Ltd who cheerfully and patiently guided me through the copyright process; Margaret McNulty and Catherine McColgan of the Institute of Irish Studies, the Queen's University of Belfast, for their unfailing support and dedication in editing this work; Val and Mary Rogers, Oxford, for their hospitality and for sharing their reminiscences of CS Lewis with me; Michael Ward, Oxford, for showing me around Lewis's former home, the Kilns; and the owners of Little Lea who generously opened their house and allowed me to view the 'little end room'.

I am grateful to thank Maurna Crozier of the Community Relations Council and the Arts Council of Northern Ireland for assistance during the research period for this work.

Introduction

Readers throughout the world normally identify CS Lewis as the author who created the imaginary world of *The Chronicles of Narnia*, the series of seven stories that began in 1950 with *The Lion, the Witch and the Wardrobe* and ended in 1956 with *The Last Battle*. They secured his reputation as one of the most popular authors in the history of children's literature. Like many readers, my own introduction to his writings came through Narnia some thirty years ago; a dozen wide-eyed schoolchildren sat cross-legged in the corner of a small County Tyrone classroom listening intently while our teacher led us through the wardrobe door, past the fur coats and, snow crunching gently underfoot, into another world.

I suspect my imaginative life started at that point; certainly it is the strongest memory of my early schooldays. Obviously I was not alone, as millions of readers across the globe and sales of *The Chronicles of Narnia* would testify. These stories touch something at the heart of our imaginative experience, something that now proves elusive to define but as a child was instinctively *felt*.

The realisation that the author of these stories was a fellow Ulsterman came to me much later and rekindled my interest in Lewis, cementing a bond that had been formed in childhood. The more works I read by and about CS Lewis, the greater his achievement as a writer became evident: an Oxford don of formidable repute, Christian apologist, broadcaster, literary critic, and to a lesser extent, a poet, science-fiction writer, and man of letters with over forty books and numerous articles to his credit. Lewis's popularity has continued to grow world-wide, helped to some degree by Sir Anthony Hopkins's sympathetic portrayal of him in the 1993 film *Shadowlands*; though close friends of the writer failed to recognise the character on the screen as the man they knew. Lewis has now achieved almost cult status, something he would have been very wary of, with books, doctoral theses, periodicals, and articles about him continuing to be published in Britain, Canada, Germany, and the United States. His work has been translated into more than twenty languages, including Welsh, Chinese, Icelandic, and even Hawaiian.

With this in mind it is ironic that one of the best selling Irish authors of all time has, until relatively recently, been somewhat neglected in his native land. The purpose of this study of CS Lewis is twofold: to explore aspects of his Irish background and influences that hitherto have not received the attention they deserve, and to consider his position as an Irish writer. Until relatively recently any question of his 'Irishness' did not arise. Lewis was considered to be a writer firmly within the canon of English literature, secure in this position by way of his reputation as a writer of children's stories and literary criticism. This perception arose, partly through his close association with the pillars of the English literary establishment – Oxford and Cambridge universities – and partly by the fact that his published works displayed little trace of his Irish influences and background.

This book attempts to rectify this and to present, for the first time in print, a detailed appraisal of Lewis's unfinished 'Ulster' novel. It is ironic that the only 'realistic' or 'modern' novel Lewis ever wrote was set in the familiar world of Belfast and should centre on the dangers inherent in the unknown world.

The unfinished novel is in many ways autobiographical: the references to the home rule debate, the social and class distinctions that governed Belfast life, and the experiences of nursing a man who was convinced he was going to hell, all had a direct relevance to his early life. That CS Lewis should describe in detail the boat journey he made between Ireland and England (up to six times a year as a student) and locate this story in his home city, Belfast, is not only an imaginative tribute to his homeland but is also the only instance in his fiction where we can discern a realistic, definable 'place'. It is fitting that that place should be Belfast and now, at the close of the centenary year of his birth, it serves as a tantalising fictional reminder of the importance CS Lewis attached to his Irish roots. If this book goes some way in helping to send readers back to Lewis's original works equipped with new perspectives on his Irish background then it will have served its purpose.

Ronald W Bresland

Chronology

1862   Birth of Florence Augusta ('Flora') Hamilton, mother of CS Lewis, in Queenstown, County Cork, Ireland, 18 May.

1863   Birth of Albert James Lewis, father of CS Lewis, in Cork, Ireland, 23 August.

1868   Lewis family move to Belfast where Richard Lewis, grandfather of CS Lewis, goes into partnership with a colleague from his Dublin workplace to found the firm of 'MacIlwaine and Lewis: Boiler Makers, Engineers, and Iron Ship Builders', at Abercorn Basin, Belfast.

1894   Marriage of Albert Lewis and Florence Hamilton at St Mark's, Dundela, Belfast, 29 August.

1895   Birth of Warren ('Warnie') Hamilton Lewis, only brother of CS Lewis, 16 June.

1898   Birth of Clive Staples Lewis, 29 November.

1905   Lewis family moves into 'Little Lea'.

1908   Death of Flora Lewis, 23 August.
       Lewis enrolled at Wynyard School, 18 September.

1910   Lewis at Campbell College, Belfast, September–November.

1911   Lewis enrolled at Cherbourg House, Malvern, January.

1914   In April, Lewis meets Arthur Greeves and the two form a close friendship that was to last for nearly fifty years.
       War declared, 4 August.
       On 19 September: Lewis meets his private tutor and fellow Ulsterman, WT Kirkpatrick at his home in Great Bookham, Surrey, and is tutored by him until March 1917.
       Lewis confirmed by his Grandfather, Rev Thomas Hamilton, at St Mark's, Dundela, on 6 December.

1917   Lewis at University College, Oxford, 29 April.
       On 8 June, Lewis joins the army and is billeted with fellow Irishman, EFC ('Paddy') Moore. Lewis introduced to Paddy's mother, Janie, on 25 September. Paddy Moore joins Rifle Brigade and is sent to France. Lewis gazetted into Somerset Light Infantry.
       On 17 November, Lewis crosses to France and arrives in Trenches on the 29 November (his nineteenth birthday).

1918   Lewis wounded in Battle of Arras, 15 April. Paddy Moore, who had been missing in action since 24 March, reported dead in the same month. Armistice signed on 11 November.

1919   Lewis returns to Oxford after a period of convalescence in English hospitals, 13 January.

Lewis's first collection of poems *Spirits in Bondage* is published, 20 March.

1921   Lewis meets WB Yeats, 14 and 21 March.

1922   Lewis takes up residence with Mrs Moore and her daughter at Headington, Oxford, 1 August.

1923   Death of Mrs Moore's brother, John Hawkins Askins, 5 April.

Lewis gains a first in English, 16 July, adding to his double first in Classics, and bringing his time at University College to an end.

1925   Lewis elected fellow of Magdalen College, 20 May.

1926   *Dymer* published, 18 September.

1929   Death of Albert Lewis, 25 September.

Lewis and Mrs Moore arrive in Belfast to clear out Little Lea. Mrs Moore stays with Arthur Greeves and his mother, 8–20 December.

Warren is still stationed in Shanghai and cannot return until the following year.

1930   Lewis and his brother at Little Lea for the last time, 23–24 April.

1931   In August, the Lewis brothers were in Ireland. During this period they visited Castlerock, County Londonderry (a favourite holiday destination from childhood), where they stayed at the Golf Hotel.

On Christmas Day, Lewis takes the necessary 'leap of faith' and proclaims his Christian conversion making his first Communion since childhood in his parish church at Headington Quarry, Oxford.

1932   Lewis writes his first prose work, *The Pilgrim's Regress*, while on holiday at Arthur Greeves's home in Belfast. Lewis also spent a few days in Kilkeel before returning to England, 15–29 August.

1933   *The Pilgrim's Regress* is published, 25 May.

The Lewis brothers arrive in Belfast to view the stained glass window in St Marks that they commissioned in memory of their parents, 8 August.

1934   Lewis, Mrs Moore, and her daughter, Maureen, take a motoring tour through parts of Ireland, stopping to visit Arthur Greeves, and allowing Mrs Moore the opportunity to meet members of the Lewis family, 31 July–31 August.

1939   War declared, 3 September

1941   Lewis gives four broadcast talks on 'Right and Wrong' on BBC, 6–27 August.

1947 In June, Lewis in Ireland for a short holiday with Arthur Greeves. This was the first time the two had met since the summer of 1938.

1950 *The Lion, the Witch and the Wardrobe* published, 16 October.

1951 Death of Mrs Moore, 12 January.
Lewis in Ireland to visit Arthur Greeves staying at The Old Inn, Crawfordsburn, County Down, a few minutes from Arthur's cottage Silverhill, 31 March–16 April.

1952 Lewis meets Joy Gresham, neé Davidman, 24 September.

1955 Lewis takes up residence in Magdalene College, Cambridge, 7 January. *Surprised by Joy* published, 19 September.

1956 Marriage of Lewis and Joy Gresham, 23 April.
During September, Lewis holidays with Arthur Greeves at Inver and Rathmullan in County Donegal.
Joy admitted to hospital suffering from cancer, 19 October.

1958 In June, after a period of recovery, Joy's cancer is diagnosed as being arrested.
In July, Lewis and Joy spend ten days in Ireland (a 'belated honeymoon') visiting counties Louth, Down and Donegal.

1959 During June and July, Lewis and Joy spend a fortnight with Arthur Greeves, before returning to Oxford on 10 July. Joy's cancer returns in October.

1960 Death of Joy Davidman Lewis, 13 July.
Lewis writes *A Grief Observed*, August.

1961 Lewis falls ill with enlarged prostrate gland, 24 June.

1963 Lewis planning to bring his stepson, Douglas, to Ireland for a holiday. Stops included Portstewart, Portballintrae, and of course, County Donegal, March–July.
Lewis admitted to hospital with heart attack, 15 July.
Death of Clive Staples Lewis, 22 November.

1966 Death of Arthur Greeves, 29 August.

1973 Death of Warren Hamilton Lewis, 9 April.

Illustrations

Sources for the illustrations are listed on page 134.

1 Belfast

The Belfast of CS Lewis's childhood was a thriving industrial city and at the beginning of the twentieth century, could lay claim to the greatest shipyard, ropeworks, tobacco factory, linen spinning mill, dry dock, and tea machinery works in the world.[1] Belfast citizens were justifiably proud of the success of their city and the young CS Lewis (known by his own choice – since the age of four – as Jack) was as enthusiastic as anyone. He remarked in later years, somewhat embarrassed by his youthful fervour, of the pleasure he and his brother Warnie gained from reminding people that Belfast had not only the largest gantry in the British Isles but had also launched the largest ship afloat, the *Oceanic*. This pride was borne out by the report in *The Freeman's Journal*, a local paper often scathing about Belfast's pretensions, when in Belfast in January 1899, the launch of the *Oceanic* was described as 'the greatest event of its kind the world has ever witnessed, and in a certain sense, perhaps the most epoch-making incident of the century'.[2] This event helped to secure Belfast's reputation as one of the leading industrial ports in Europe. Lewis was just six weeks old when the *Oceanic* was launched and the effect of a childhood spent within earshot of the great industrial heart of Belfast moved him to declare that 'the sound of a steamer's horn at night still conjures up my whole boyhood'.[3]

The dawn of the new century saw Belfast emerge as the most economically successful city in Ireland, and if its citizens shared in the satisfaction of their city's growing prosperity and reputation, the old barriers of religion, class, and politics still had the power to divide them. Warnie Lewis sums up the gulf between the two dominant religions in Belfast when commenting on the death of Joe Devlin,[4] a Roman Catholic politician and friend of his father, who held one of the four Nationalist seats in Belfast. To the best of his knowledge, Warnie asserts that Joe Devlin was the only Catholic politician who was 'persona grata' with the Protestant ascendancy without deviating from his own firmly-held political beliefs, a rare event that he attributes solely to Devlin's 'honesty and charm'. He goes on to say that in 1930s Belfast you would be more likely 'to meet a Papist in social intercourse with a Protestant than you would be to find in France a Bonapartist at the table of a Legitimist'.[5]

It was not only religion that divided Belfast society. Jack Lewis was fortunate to have been born into a family that enjoyed many of the advantages of the middle classes: relative financial security, a comfortable home, annual seaside holidays, and servants – including a gardener, a nursemaid, a governess, a cook, and a housemaid. The Lewis family had previously lived in the more densely-populated area of Dundela where they rented a semi-detached villa from Albert Lewis's brother-in-law, Thomas Keown, until moving to a new house, 'Little Lea' in 1905.

The Lewis family's decision to build a large private residence in the affluent Strandtown/Belmont area of east Belfast was motivated partly by concern for the health of their two sons. A report into the state of public health in Belfast conducted in 1906 found that the annual death rate from tuberculosis was more than double that of England and Wales, and worse than that of Dublin. Poor sanitary conditions resulted in Belfast having the highest death rate from typhoid in the United Kingdom.

Apart from these concerns, the Lewis family was determined to advance within the social hierarchy. Jack's father, Albert Lewis, was the first of the family to enter the learned professions. He was educated at the Model School, Belfast and afterwards at Lurgan College and Queen's College, Belfast (now the Queen's University of Belfast). He was then apprenticed as a solicitor to the firm of McLean, Boyle, and McLean, at 45 Arthur Street, Belfast, close to the premises where the *Belfast Telegraph* was published before it transferred to Royal Avenue in 1886. The head of the firm of solicitors was James McLean, who was for many years Sessional Crown Solicitor in Belfast and whose son was prosecutor for the Belfast Corporation (it was on the latter's appointment as a Resident Magistrate that Albert Lewis was chosen as his replacement in 1890). After finishing his apprenticeship, which included training in Dublin, and being admitted as a solicitor in the Trinity term of 1885, Albert Lewis went into practice with WH Arbuthnot. That partnership was subsequently dissolved and he eventually established his own practice at 83 Royal Avenue, Belfast.

Albert was sensitive to the class distinctions that governed the social and economic life of the city and aspired to integrate fully into the upper echelons of that society. By building a large private residence (smaller than, but symbolic of, the 'big house' so favoured by generations of the ascendancy class), in one of the most exclusive areas of Belfast, Albert Lewis was making a definitive social statement. Having secured a wife from a socially distinguished family he felt, to a certain extent, the need to prove his worth and the new house, named Leeborough or Little Lea, was the outward display of his success. His neighbours were some of the most wealthy people in Belfast and included Captain James Craig (later Lord Craigavon and the first Prime Minister of Northern Ireland), Gustav Wilhelm Wolff (partner in Harland & Wolff shipyard) and Archibald Dunlap Lemon (son of a local shipowner and director of the Ulster Steamship Company). That Albert could rise from relatively humble origins to live among some of the 'most substantial people'[6] in the city is a testament to his ambition and industry. Albert was initially preoccupied with financial worries and it appears that he was prepared to weather the cost of maintaining such a lifestyle to retain social respectability. A striking monument to class divisions can be seen in the *Titanic* memorial at City Hall, Belfast, where the names of local people who perished on the ship's maiden voyage in April 1912 are listed, not in alphabetical order as is common with the war dead, but in order of social rank, with the wealthiest given prominence. This is a grim reminder of just how deeply these distinctions permeated the social order.[7]

While CS Lewis would comment in later years that, 'as a social historian I am sounder on Toad Hall ... than on London, Oxford, and Belfast',[8] Sybil Gribbon has noted that:

The hierarchy of class dominated Edwardian [Belfast] society. At its apex were the three hundred families, whose households at Strandtown or on the high ridges of the Antrim and Malone Roads contained a gardener and coachman as well as several indoor servants ... They were in many ways a tight-knit group: the men meeting daily for lunch in the Ulster or Reform Clubs and in the board rooms of the town's interlocking companies, or at weekends playing golf together and sailing at Cultra; their wives visiting rarely outside their own circle; their children, educated in English schools, dancing and playing tennis at each other's houses, welding more firmly in their marriages the commercial oligarchy of the town.[9]

While the Lewis family were not among the select elite that helped shape and develop industrial Belfast they certainly gravitated towards that social environment: Albert Lewis was a political speaker of some importance within the Conservative party in Belfast – he was the principal speaker at a meeting of Sir James Corry's[10] supporters held in Belfast in October 1885 – and was a witty and able advocate of Conservative policies.[11] As with many of the aspiring Protestant middle classes he was also a member of one the exclusive men's clubs, the Union Club, in Belfast and afforded their most prominent citizens the opportunity to meet and discuss issues close to their hearts.

The literary temperament that runs through the Lewis family can be seen in the early letters from Albert to his first love Edie Macown, when he was eighteen, informing her of the local Belmont Literary Society of which he had just become a member. After explaining the operations of the society, he added – with no obvious pretension – that he was considered one of their best orators. The similarities between father and son are here apparent when we consider that Jack was also attracted to organised literary debate among male friends, as can be seen from his close association with the Oxford groups, the Martlets, and later the Inklings, where he read aloud from his current works in the company of friends and fellow members such as JRR Tolkien and Charles Williams.

The Belmont Literary Society allowed Albert an outlet to express his literary aspirations and to develop his rhetorical ability. It appears that Albert was also using his relationship with Edie Macown to sharpen his literary style. Warnie Lewis, while editing his father's letters, notes 'the draft replies ... are so literary in their form as to lead us to expect that in this boy and girl love affair he was rather "in love with love" than with his Edie'.[12] We find the same impulse to perfect literary expression in the young CS Lewis's letters to his friend, Arthur Greeves, where the letters tend at times to resemble critical essays rather than personal correspondence, an aspect which Lewis recognised when he recalled later, with an appalled amusement, his own 'prigishness' at this time. Whether what follows is an example of Albert's literary flair or an elaborate attempt to disentangle himself from his beloved Edie, we do not know. Writing to Edie, he informed her of his visit to an aged phrenologist who was lecturing in Belfast with the intention of getting the man to 'read my head'. The old man revealed that Albert would not make a good lawyer and, more to the point, that he was inclined to become infatuated with girls, thinking himself in love with them, when in fact he had yet to meet any girl with whom he could settle down 'to love truly and sincerely'. The letter ends with fervent thanks for her 'last' letter with Albert vowing to 'cherish it till it drops to pieces with continual reading'.[13] Warnie, as editor of the family papers, wrote underneath this entry, 'the letter in question is as fresh and unfrayed as the day the paper was first folded'. What became of Edie we do not know, for shortly afterwards she disappears from the records, after a courtship of five years.

By the time Albert began courting the daughter of the local rector, Florence Hamilton, his social expectations were somewhat higher and his first faltering steps on the road to social advancement were taken with a self-conscious trepidation. The following comment by Warnie Lewis in 1921 reveals something of the social climate at the time: 'Today I read Frank Frankfort Moore's *The*

*A family group c 1900 showing both parents and three grandparents. Front row (l. to r.):
Florence (Flora) Lewis, Jack's mother, Warren Augustus ('Gussie') Hamilton (uncle),
Anne Hamilton (aunt) and the Rev Thomas Hamilton (grandfather). Back row (l. to r.):
Albert Lewis (father), Mary Hamilton (grandmother), Richard Lewis (grandfather) and
an unidentified clergyman.*

Ulsterman ... It is a biting exposure of North of Ireland life showing up under
thinly veiled names the more prominent Belfastians of the last generation.
Their hypocrisy, snobbery, and determination to get on, their sneers at each
other's ancestors and their bigotry are all most amusingly exposed.'[14] That
Albert should have been somewhat sensitive regarding the Hamilton family is
understandable considering that the girl he hoped to marry was related to one
of the wealthiest families in Belfast. Florence Hamilton's cousin and closest
friend was Lady Ewart, wife of Sir William Quartus Ewart, the wealthy Belfast
linen manufacturer and one of the city's most prominent industrialists. Later, it
was at their opulent mansion, Glenmachan,[15] less than a mile from Little Lea,
that the Lewis boys had a standing invitation to visit while home from school
in England, and it was to this hospitality that Jack credited whatever courtesy

and *savoir faire* he and Warnie possessed. Though comparable to life at Little Lea in many ways, assured wealth afforded a lifestyle that eluded the Lewis family. Jack's subtle distinction sums up the gulf: 'Life there was more spacious and considered than with us, glided like a barge where ours bumped like a cart.'[16]

The sophistication and affluence of such an environment was an intimidating prospect for one outside its arena and Albert Lewis was initially extremely sensitive about his place within the hierarchy. His ancestors had been Welsh farmers and his father, Richard, moved to Ireland in the 1850s, working for the Cork Steamship Company before moving to Dublin to take up a better job with another shipbuilding firm in 1864, when Albert was one year old. Jack Lewis paid tribute to this Celtic link when he said: 'I'm more Welsh than anything ... and for more than anything else in my ancestry I'm grateful that on my father's side I'm descended from a practical Welsh farmer. To that link with the soil I owe whatever measure of physical energy and stability I have. Without it I should have turned into a hopeless neurotic.'[17]

In 1868 the family moved to Belfast, where Richard went into partnership with a colleague from his Dublin workplace to found the firm of 'MacIlwaine and Lewis: Boiler Makers, Engineers, and Iron Ship Builders', at Abercorn Basin, Belfast.[18] However, politics and class remained an obstacle for a self-made entrepreneur with a working class background. Writing in May 1883, Albert cautioned his father against entering into a proposed business scheme in Larne due to the bipartisan nature of the harbour commissioners who controlled the port (or rather the 'clique' of committees who control their 'brethren'). Albert added that if the 'bigotry, the aggrandisement, and the parsimony of the Conservative GENTLEMEN of Belfast' were an example of the teachings of that party then he would almost be inclined 'to turn his coat' and align himself with rampant radicalism.[19] The partnership between McIlwaine and Lewis was now coming under strain from another quarter, and Albert was convinced that the row brewing between both partners was class motivated and stemmed from the fact that John McIlwaine, encouraged by his wife, considered being on the same social footing as Richard Lewis (as their business 'partnership' necessarily implied), something of a disgrace!

Richard Lewis had strong working-class roots and was instrumental in forming one of the first working-men's co-operative societies in Cork in the 1860s with the express intention of advancing the educational and social life of workers in the area. He wrote numerous essays of a theological nature and gave papers advocating the benefits of education to the Cork Steamship Company's

working-men's reading rooms, where he worked. Richard Lewis's sincere egal-
itarianism is evident in the many speeches he gave to his fellow workers, where
he advocated the numerous benefits to be gained from reading, study, and
equally as important, the abstention from alcohol. When not berating his fellow
workers for their intemperance, Richard would, for his own amusement, com-
pose fantasy stories to amuse his children with titles such as 'The Curse of St
Multose'.[20] His desire to direct people 'on the right path' and his literary bent
foreshadow the interests that his grandson, CS Lewis, was to develop to such
effect in later years.

When Albert began courting Florence Hamilton he was in no doubt that he
was aspiring to rise 'above his station' in hoping to marry her. He was stung by
a condescending remark made by Flora's sister, Lillian, concerning 'family'.
Flora responded by trying to ally Albert's concerns, diplomatically pointing out
that they could have a comfortable life together and as far as luxuries were concerned, they were little more than 'social display' and not worth the bother.
Florence Hamilton's family had a distinguished ancestry that included 'many
generations of clergymen, lawyers, sailors, and the like ... and on her mother's
side, through the Warrens, the blood went back to a Norman knight whose
bones lie at Battle Abbey'.[21] In class-conscious Belfast society, social distinctions were an important consideration in marital decisions; Flora attended
'Ladies Classes' in Methodist College, Belfast, which were an integral part of
preparing young ladies for marital duties within their own social class. The
Hamiltons had the quiet confidence in their ancestry that bred a certain self-
assuredness and when young Jack Lewis wrote his first stories declaring 'they
were an attempt to combine my two chief literary pleasures – "dressed
animals" and "knights-in-armour" ',[22] it was in part an imaginative tribute
and acknowledgement of the family's proud association with this noble
ancestor.[23]

The Hamilton family regarded Albert as perhaps not quite the 'catch' they
had hoped for their daughter, but the young man was obviously in love with
Flora and, more importantly, had relatively good social and financial prospects
as a solicitor or perhaps a politician. While they considered Albert 'only just a
gentleman' (having, as it were, a less illustrious pedigree than the Hamiltons)
they were not averse to manipulating Albert's romantic attachment to their
daughter.

Rev Thomas Hamilton, Flora's father, was the worst offender, engaging
Albert as a companion on the various jaunts of which he was so fond. Warnie
notes that his father's youth and his somewhat 'ambiguous' social status in

Rev Thomas Hamilton, rector of St Mark's Dundela, 1878–1900, grandfather of CS Lewis.

comparison to grandfather Hamilton gave rise to an 'inferiority complex' which manifested itself in Albert's rather exaggerated behaviour. This was characterised by a readiness to please that extended to his paying of tips, however large, without objection, and an emphasis on manners that bordered on the ridiculous. This generous tendency in his daughter's suitor pleased Thomas Hamilton greatly, until there was a hitch in their travel arrangements, when camaraderie gave way to rancorous lamentations that shamed the sensitive Albert to the very soul. On one occasion Thomas Hamilton stamped up and down the crowded platform at Euston, declaiming loudly, 'Alas, they had been friends in youth', with a vigour which was remembered by Albert with horror more than thirty years later.[24] Albert's marriage to Flora in 1894 ended these purgatorial holidays, a fact which his new father-in-law was quick to recognise, characteristically remarking at the wedding: 'Now he's got what he wanted, there'll be no more jaunts.'

In his autobiography, *Surprised by Joy*, CS Lewis said of his family, 'Two

Family group c 1900. Front row (l. to r.): Mary Hamilton (cousin) on her father Warren Augustus ('Gussie') Hamilton's knee, Martha Lewis (grandmother), Albert Lewis with his sons Warnie and Jack on his knee and Anne Hamilton (aunt). Back row (l. to r.): Richard Lewis (grandfather), Eileen Lewis (cousin), Flora Lewis (mother), Leonard Lewis (cousin) and Agnes Lewis (aunt).

very different strains had gone to our making'. He was referring to his Saxon and Celtic ancestry and the concomitant differences in origin and temperament between the two. Lewis says of his lineage:

My father's people were true Welshmen, sentimental, passionate, and rhetorical, easily moved both to anger and to tenderness; men who laughed and cried a great deal and who had not much of the talent for happiness. The Hamilton's were a cooler race. Their minds were critical and ironic and they had the talent for happiness in a high degree – went straight for it as experienced travellers go for the best seat in a train.[25]

From an early age, Jack was aware of the vivid contrast between his mother's 'cheerful and tranquil affection', and his father's volatile temperament. This bred in him a distrust of emotion as something, 'uncomfortable and embarrassing and even dangerous'. The perceived conflict between these views owes much to the writings of Matthew Arnold and James Anthony Froude, who advanced racial theories on the nature of the Celtic temperament. Froude speaks of the Celtic race as being:

Light-hearted, humorous, imaginative, susceptible through the entire range of feeling, from the profoundest pathos to the most playful jest ... Passionate in everything – passionate in their patriotism, passionate in their religion, passionately courageous, passionately loyal and affectionate, they are without the manliness which will give strength and solidity to the sentimental part of their dispositions, while the surface and show is so seductive and so winning that only experience of its instability can resist the charm.[26]

Jack's instinctive uneasiness with his father's volatile Celtic temperament bred in him not only a distrust and dislike of emotion but a fear of his father that invariably created a barrier in their future relations. However, these feelings only surfaced following the death of his mother in 1908, and Jack's early years at Dundela Villas and Little Lea were extremely happy ones. Despite Jack and Warnie's awareness that their father was prone to moodiness, their remarkably contented life at this time was summed up by Jack as containing everything a child needs: 'good parents, good food, and a garden to play in'.

One of the highlights of the year for the boys was the annual seaside holidays with their mother, normally to Castlerock but also visiting Portrush and Ballycastle, where they would stay for up to six weeks at a time. This was a regular feature of middle-class life in Ulster and it was one of the privileges of a relatively secure financial background that the family could afford to take an extended holiday rather than the usual day trip or weekend break. Albert usually excused himself from the family holiday by declaring that he had urgent business to attend to, and would confine his visits during these periods to the occasional weekend. Warnie's abiding memory of these holidays was the contrast between the family's excitement and preparation for the holiday and his father's gloomy detachment. He adds:

I never met a man more wedded to a dull routine, or less capable of extracting enjoyment from life. A night spent out of the house was a penance to him: a holiday he loathed, having not the faintest conception of how to amuse himself. I can still see him on his occasional visits to the seaside, walking moodily up and down the beach, hands in trouser pockets, eyes on the ground, every now and then giving a heartrending yawn and pulling out his watch.[27]

These holidays instilled in Jack a sense of the geography of Ulster and the wider landscape which he was to incorporate into his childhood stories and drawings: we can see that his earliest writings were coloured by his environment. His stories of 'Animal-Land' which, when combined with his brother's stories on 'India', coalesced into the singular world they named Boxen. The stories feature various anthropomorphic characters but should not be seen as an early model for the Narnian chronicles for which Lewis was to be best known. What distinguishes the Animal-Land and Boxen stories from the Narnian ones, is first, their prosaic nature: Lewis asserted that their whole quality 'excluded the least hint of wonder'.[28] Second, the Animal-Land and Boxen stories differed from the Narnian chronicles in that they all had a *political* framework: these dressed mice, rabbits, and frogs inhabited the everyday world, not an imaginative one.

These stories combine politics, history and a certain realism that reflects Jack's childlike attentiveness to the adult world and his keen ear for realistic dialogue. The home rule debate and talk of the proposed establishment of a separate parliament in Dublin would have been issues that were hotly discussed in the Lewis household and inevitably found their way into the young boy's imagination. Commenting on the symbolic and artistic union of Jack's Animal-Land and Warnie's India into the single state of Boxen, Lewis writes:

By a wise provision they retained their separate kings but had a common legislative assembly, the Damerfesk ... The electoral system was democratic, but this mattered very much less than in England, for the Damerfesk was never doomed to one fixed meeting place ... The records sometimes call this assembly the Parliament, but this is misleading. It only had a single chamber, and the kings presided.[29]

This fragment displays a remarkable maturity and grasp of political systems for a boy aged eight or nine and not only reinforces the seriousness and sense of purpose that young Jack applied to his work but reflects the assimilation of the political sensibilities of his immediate environment that led him to announce to his grandfather, to the amusement of the family, that he was, 'a Home-Ruler'.[30] The stories are given an added dimension by the comprehensive use of maps and drawings to further enliven this elaborate world populated by, among others, an aristocratic frog, a rabbit king, and an artistic owl. In mapping and chronicling these imaginary worlds Jack declared he was 'training myself to be a novelist. Note well, a novelist; not a poet'.[31]

The impulse towards mapping imaginary landscapes is something that Jack was to refine and develop in his later works. He uses maps in *The Pilgrim's*

Regress and the Narnian books to guide the reader through the mental landscape of his creations; to give the imagined world a more concrete and vivid
embodiment. The symbolism of 'North' and 'South' in these invented worlds
can be used to distinguish between many varieties of experience and is not
confined merely to geographical terrain. In *The Pilgrim's Regress*, he uses this
system to differentiate between 'Northerners ... the men of rigid systems
whether sceptical or dogmatic ... signed and sealed members of highly
organised "Parties" ' while the 'Southerners' are characterised as being

> ... less definable; boneless souls whose doors stand open day and night to almost every
> visitant, but almost with readiest welcome for those ... who offer some sort of intoxi-
> cation. The delicious tang of the forbidden and the unknown draws them on with fatal
> attraction ... Every feeling is justified by the mere fact that it is felt: for a Northerner,
> every feeling on the same ground is suspect.[32]

He applied this criteria to people as early as 1909 when he said of his school
friend, 'Now Boivie is a Swede, and therefore a good Northerner, and like us,
hates anything that savours of the South of England.'[33] These distinctions of
type are not an allusion to the inhabitants of his native land but herald the development of one of the most influential discoveries of his childhood – the concept of Northernness. Lewis was utterly captivated by Norse mythology and the
music of Richard Wagner, which liberated and transformed his imagination.
They evoked in him a dim and distant memory of something he felt he had
experienced before, a memory of a time at Dundela Villas when Warnie had
presented him with a toy garden made from moss and leaves in an old biscuit
tin, that triggered a feeling of bliss, that was tinged with a delectable longing:
what he would later come to define as *joy*. Jack also realised that these
epiphanies revealed 'the supreme and only important object of desire'.[34]

  Lewis could not identify this sensation of joy until much later. The effect of
this revelation on his imagination cannot be overestimated for it informs much
of his later thought and cleared the way for his eventual acceptance of
Christianity. The religious significance of the toy garden, with its connotations
of the Garden of Eden, and the feeling evoked that Lewis was 'returning at last
from exile and desert lands to my own country' are loaded with biblical symbolism and suggest that even at this young age he had absorbed something
valuable from the Christianity of his upbringing. After Jack had embraced
Christianity in later life he would recognise these early events as being spiritual manifestations, not the thing itself: 'not the wave but the waves imprint on

The young CS Lewis, photographed at Glenmachan, Belfast.

the sand'.[35] However, it was to be many years before he fully understood the importance of these spiritual pointers.

That these experiences were mediated through nature goes some way to explaining the attachment Jack had with his homeland. It is in the combination of his poetic sensibility and affinity with the Irish landscape that we see Lewis emerging as a topographer of the imagination. This in turn allowed him to embrace the concept of *Northernness*, intellectually and spiritually, that was to have such a profound effect on his thought. He tried, tentatively, to put into words this elusive sensation and compared it to 'a vision of huge, clear spaces hanging above the Atlantic in the endless twilight of Northern summer, remoteness, severity ... and almost at the same moment I knew that I had met this before, long, long ago ...'[36] He goes on to equate this intense revelation with the feelings of a man returning from exile and desert lands to his true homeland.

Whether Jack was aware that the local landscape he inhabited also bore the marks of Norse influence is not known. Carlingford and Strangford loughs both owe their names to the Vikings: undoubtedly the imaginative connection between Norse influence and his local landscape is something that would have inspired him. The impulse to reinvent and reinterpret experience imaginatively was something that Lewis was to frequently employ in his attitudes to Ireland.

Overshadowing CS Lewis's early life in Belfast was the anxiety caused by the political events of the period, which tended to permeate the social and domestic life of the household. As the home rule debate rumbled on, talk at Little Lea inevitably revolved around politics. Warnie sums up life at Leeborough thus:

In the upper-middle class society of our Belfast childhood, politics and money were the chief, almost the only, subjects of grown-up conversation: and since no visitors came to our house who did not hold precisely the same political views as my father, what we heard was not discussion and the lively clash of minds, but rather an endless and one-sided torrent of grumble and vituperation. Any ordinary parent would have sent us boys off to amuse ourselves, but not my father: we had to sit in silence and endure it. The immediate result, in Jack's case, was to convince him that grown-up conversation and politics were one in the same thing, and that everything he wrote must therefore be given a political framework: the longterm result was to fill him with a disgust and revulsion from the very idea of politics before he was out of his teens.[37]

The idea that no discussion took place other than with people who held 'precisely the same political views' is, however, somewhat disingenuous. Warnie

has perhaps forgotten to take into account the views of his maternal grandmother, Mary Hamilton, who remained a vocal and committed supporter of
home rule all her life. She was in total opposition to the political views of her
husband, Rev Thomas Hamilton, and was regarded as somewhat eccentric by
other members of the family. Her grandson gives the following account of calling at the rectory at St Mark's, Dundela:

The house was typical of the woman: infested with cats ... their presence was immediately apparent to the nose of the visitor when the slatternly servant opened the front door.
Supposing himself to have been invited to dine he would find himself in a dirty drawing
room, adorned with rare specimens of glass, china and silver. The hand which his host-
ess extended to him would gleam with valuable rings, but would bear too evident traces
of her enthusiasm as a poultry keeper. The announcement of dinner was the signal for a
preconcerted rush on the part of the family, the object of which was to ensure the unfortunate guest the chair which had only three sound legs. The dinner ... was likely to
be in keeping with the general style of the establishment, and the visitor, having partaken
of a perfectly cooked salmon off a chipped kitchen dish, would probably be offered an
execrably mangled chop, served on a collector's piece of Sheffield plate.[38]

Besides turning the rectory into something resembling an establishment out of
the pages of Somerville and Ross, she did not endear herself to her Protestant
neighbours by employing Catholic servants from southern Ireland. What
Warnie found remarkable, and admirable, about his grandmother was that she,
an 'ardent Nationalist' and member of a distinguished Protestant ascendancy
family from the south of Ireland, could openly hold and articulate such
opinions in Belfast.

In a letter to her on the question of home rule, Albert questioned the nature
of the Irish character to confront the turbulence and inefficiency he saw inherent in Grattan's parliament, and feared that any new parliament would be
marred by these old faults. Nevertheless, he conceded: 'everything that is
occurring around us points to the conclusion that the experiment must be
tried'.[39] Mary replied that while she agreed with Albert that men of undoubted
honesty would take opposite views, the cause of this would be ignorance arising out of want of study of a complicated subject. Then, in a spirited argument
in favour of home rule in which she brands the English as an 'alien robber
crew', Mary asserts that it is 'not to be accepted without trial that God made
Irishmen as a special crooked pattern particularly to plague Englishmen and
exercise their great qualities'.[40] She concludes that self-government would be
as beneficial to Ireland as it had been to other countries.

While these were the opinions of both parties in 1885, Albert hardened his position somewhat as the home rule crisis developed in following years. Thereafter, the official attitude within the Lewis family was to regard Mary's home rule convictions as a 'laughable eccentricity'.[41] Perhaps gender politics and the spirit of the age help to explain the condescending attitude towards Mrs Hamilton as much as her supposed 'eccentricity'. The idea that Jack had a violent dislike of politics while still a teenager does not really tell the full story either. We know that CS Lewis attempted to write an 'Ulster novel' in his late twenties.[42] It is an essay written by Jack in 1908, entitled 'Home Rule', however, which reveals the extent of his grasp of the Irish political situation. In it he states that he will defend home rule when he grows up while also acknowledging that it is a 'matter of mighty weight not to be answered in a moment'. The short essay concludes with the young author echoing grandmother Hamilton's sentiments, posing the question, 'What would you do with Home Rule if you got it?' The reply, 'what we will do with [it] is our business but we would do a great deal more than you would like', strikes Jack as being 'a pretty smart answer I think'.[43] The ability to balance opposing arguments, together with an appreciation of the humour involved, is evident in this early fragment and represents a remarkable achievement for a boy of his age. In another sense, it also reveals an early example of Jack's opinions departing from his father's and beginning to assert his own personality through his writing.

One of the greatest advantages for a young boy with a literary temperament is to be born into a family that engages in, and actively encourages, literary pursuits. If, at the beginning of the twentieth century, Belfast could lay claim to being 'the most literate corner of Ireland'[44] then the Lewis household was an extravagant testimony to the veracity of this. Jack said of Little Lea:

There were books in the study, books in the drawing-room, books in the cloakroom, books (two deep) in the great bookcase on the landing, books in a bedroom, books piled as high as my shoulder in the cistern attic, books of all kinds reflecting every transient stage of my parents' interests, books readable and unreadable, books suitable for a child and books most emphatically not. Nothing was forbidden me. In the seemingly endless rainy afternoons I took volume after volume from the shelves. I had always the same certainty of finding a book that was new to me as a man who walks into a field has of finding a new blade of grass.[45]

Albert Lewis kept an account at Mullan's bookshop at Castle Junction, Belfast, and would often take his sons there. It was run by a man called 'little Carson' with whom Albert built up a great friendship over the 55 years he was a patron, and a visit to Mullan's was more like a social occasion than a shopping expedition. Warnie remembers that when he and Jack visited the shop with their father at Christmas, they were allowed to choose a new book each as a present. In considering the bookish environment that Jack Lewis was brought up in and his own literary temperament, there seems a sort of inevitability that he should become a writer. Lewis's childhood ambition to be a novelist had led him to collaborate with Warnie to produce the Animal-Land and Boxen stories. Writing to his close friend, Arthur Greeves, in 1930 it is evident, however, that he had abandoned his earlier ambition to be a novelist and was concentrating his energies on becoming a poet instead. He confides, 'From the age of sixteen onwards I had one single ambition, from which I never wavered, in the prosecution of which I spent every ounce I could, on which I really and deliberately staked my whole contentment ...'[46]

The influence of Jack's immediate family circle was instrumental in shaping these literary aspirations and provided him with an enthusiastic and receptive audience. His parents and grandparents were all involved, to some degree, in composing either stories, poems, speeches, or journals, and they all shared their literary attempts with other members of the family. A significant aspect of this was that many of these works were written with the intent of being read aloud to other family members. Warnie, commenting on his grandfather's dedication to recording his travel experiences, notes that the journals were 'marred throughout by the strivings of a young man after a richness of style which it was not within the compass of his talent to achieve; the purpose of their production explains, though it cannot excuse, his "precious element", "heaving billows", and all the other horrors of his abominably affected style'.[47]

Jack Lewis was to benefit greatly from the experience of articulating his thoughts in front of the family audience. Tapping into the Irish oral tradition of storytelling, he knew how to hold an audience's attention, entertain, and communicate in plain language. His influential book, *Mere Christianity*, for instance, was originally a series of broadcast talks given for the BBC to bolster the troops during the Second World War. When Lewis came to edit these talks for publication he found he had very little rewriting to do because his writing style reflected his confidence in the spoken word, or as he succinctly put it: 'If you cannot put your faith in the vernacular then either you don't know it or you don't believe it.'[48]

If grandfather Hamilton had lacked rhetorical finesse then Albert Lewis had no such shortcomings. Having received certificates of merit for his 'proficiency in vocal music'[49] at the local national school, he went on to become a skilled

Detail from a photograph taken on the graduation day of Flora Lewis at the Queen's University of Belfast in 1886. Flora Lewis is seated in the front row, extreme left.

prosecuting solicitor and possessed, among many attributes 'a fine presence, a resonant voice, great quickness of mind, eloquence and memory'.[50] Jack described him as the best raconteur he had ever heard and praised his ability to act all the characters of his story with a liberal use of grimace, gesture, and pantomime.

Jack's parents had both harboured literary aspirations. Albert's early stories were purely imitative of 'Captain' Frederick Marryat's seafaring yarns, with rousing titles such as 'James's Adventure', 'The Runaway Boy', and 'Frank Fearless', to match his favourite author's predilection for stirring titles. Among his literary productions were the stories 'Major Smith and Mr Pie', 'The story of the Half Sovereign', 'The Law's an Ass', and the story rejected by *Titbits* in 1890, 'A Penny in the Slot'. We know that Albert considered writing an auto-biography but nothing came of the idea. The following fragmentary outline may have been a draft idea for a story similar to the previous compositions but it is hard to resist seeing it as tentatively autobiographical. It reads 'The Lea … The House … the family, especially the head … a man of genius, but full of nerves … drifting to drink, not because he likes it but because it stills his agitation. Head of great firm … religious man … etc'.[51]

It is significant that the caricature of Albert Lewis that appears in *Ireland's Saturday Night* newspaper in 1921 shows him holding a mortar board under one arm and a volume entitled *English Literature* under the other: the significance being that he was apparently as well known as a literary man as he was as a solicitor. His obituary in the *Belfast Telegraph* noted:

The unostentatious aspects of the late Mr Lewis were to a certain extent known to his intimates, but he had an instinctive repugnance to allowing his acts to become known, and it might truly be said of him that 'he did good by stealth and blushed to find it fame.' A well read and erudite man, he found his chief recreation away from the courts of law in reading, and the classical and standard authors had in him a student of cultivated taste and deep appreciation.[52]

Florence Lewis shared Albert's love of literature while also displaying a remarkable aptitude for mathematics, and was among the first women to graduate from the Queen's University of Belfast, in 1886, taking a first in logic and a second class honours degree in mathematics. She also fared better in her literary attempts and succeeded, where her husband had failed, in getting a story, 'The Princess Rosetta,' published in the London magazine, *The Household Journal*. It is not surprising therefore that both parents should encourage their children's literary and imaginative development; such activities were an

A caricature of Albert Lewis, Ireland's Saturday Night , *1921. It is accompanied by the following verse:*

> *If the world of letters were upside down,*
> *And books of quotations were no more to hand,*
> *Mr. A.J. Lewis would still 'meet the case'*
> *With the choicest of 'gems' at his tongue's command*

integral feature of the family's daily life and formed habits that Jack and Warnie adhered to throughout their lives. Evidence of this support can be seen in 'The Leeborough Review', a manuscript weekly of which Albert appears to be chief critic and editor. In issue five, written in January 1912, Albert praises 'Mr C. S. Lewis's' new musical comedy, 'The Jester's Tale', though adding that 'a musical absurdity' would be a better definition of the work, and singles out the character 'Poshes', 'a gloomy individual who under the cloak of pompous disregard for idle jestings conceals an inability to grasp the simplest witticism',[53] as the star of the play. Albert, apparently oblivious to this thinly-veiled reference to himself, goes on to praise the various characters and hopes the author will maintain his high standards. We see Jack expressing his increasing frustration with his father by turning him into a character in the play. That Albert should single out 'Poshes' as the 'star' of the piece without any comprehension that the character was based on him shows the widening gulf in relations between them.

The barrier between son and father was something that perplexed Jack throughout his life and the relationship ranged from barely-concealed resentment to comic absurdity. As we shall see, Jack led a double life that hinged on concealing certain facts from his father and this habit caused him not only a certain amount of guilt but some awkward moments.

More often, though, the misunderstandings between them were simply bizarre. For instance, a certain church in Belfast has both a Greek inscription over the door and a curious tower. 'That church is a great landmark. I can pick it out from all sorts of places – even from the top of Cave Hill' said Jack, to which Albert replied, 'Such nonsense, how could you make out Greek letters three or four miles away?'[54] Jack's account of his father in *Surprised by Joy* gives an impression of Albert Lewis that, while certainly very entertaining, is somewhat distorted. The Albert Lewis who emerges from the pages of *The Lewis Papers*, the history of the family, is a more complex figure and has a greater influence on his son's development as a writer than the autobiography suggests.

2 Souls to Possess

In 1908, the tranquil existence at Little Lea was shattered by the death of Florence Lewis from a long and protracted battle with abdominal cancer, and was a traumatic event for the young Lewis brothers. For Albert, Flora's death was an even more devastating blow, and one from which he never really recovered. As well as losing his wife in August, two weeks later he also lost his elder brother, Joseph, while his father had died in April of that same year. For young Jack, the death of his mother was a terrifying experience, and in his autobiography *Surprised by Joy*, he describes, not only the fear of losing his mother, but the pivotal change in attitude towards his father:

Children suffer not (I think) less than their elders, but differently. For us boys the real bereavement had happened before our mother died. We lost her gradually as she was gradually withdrawn from our life into the hands of nurses and delirium and morphia, and as our whole existence changed into something alien and menacing, as the house became full of strange smells and midnight noises and sinister whispered conversations. This had two further results, one very evil and one very good. It divided us from our father as well as our mother. They say that a shared sorrow draws people closer together; I can hardly believe that it often has that effect when those that share it are of widely different ages. If I may trust to my own experience, the sight of adult misery and adult terror has an effect on children that is merely paralysing and alienating. Perhaps it was our fault. Perhaps if we had been better children we might have lightened our father's sufferings at this time. We certainly did not.[1]

The overriding experience of his mother's death can be summed up in the phrase that Jack was to write over forty years later and in depressingly similar circumstances, when he observed, 'no one told me that grief felt so like fear'.[2] His life-long aversion to displays of adult grief was fixed by the trauma of his mother's death and is vividly illustrated when he asked, 'Where in all nature is there anything uglier and more undignified than an adult male face blubbered and distorted with weeping?'[3] Returning to the autobiography, we see the pain and resentment still evident in his feelings towards his father:

His nerves had never been of the steadiest and his emotions had always been uncontrolled. Under the pressure of anxiety his temper became incalculable; he spoke wildly and acted unjustly. Thus by a peculiar cruelty of fate, during those months the unfortunate man, had he but known it, was losing his sons as well as his wife. We were coming, my brother and I, to rely more and more exclusively on each other for all that made life bearable; to have confidence only in each other. I expect that we (or at any rate I) were already learning to lie to him. Everything that had made the house a home had failed us; everything except one another. We drew daily closer together (that was the good result) ... two frightened urchins huddled for warmth in a bleak world.[4]

The pathos in the last line may be intended to elicit our sympathy for the boys' plight or a final broadside to emphasise Albert's failure as a father. It is clear that the whole experience fractured family relationships to such an extent that reconciliation became extremely difficult. Jack saw himself as being very much on his own from this point and summed it up thus: 'With my mother's death all settled, happiness, all that was tranquil and reliable, disappeared from my life. There was to be much fun, many pleasures, many stabs of Joy; but no more of the old security. It was sea and islands now; the great continent had sunk like Atlantis.'[5]

Within two weeks of his mother's death, Jack returned with his brother to England to attend Wynyard House boarding school in Watford, where Warnie was already a pupil. Any greater wrench is hard to imagine: a young grieving boy sent off, within a fortnight of his mother's death, to a strange country and an even stranger school (the headmaster was later put under restraint and certified insane). Albert, in sending Jack to a public school, had hoped to, 'break down his shyness ... his morbid desire for isolation and seclusion, which has been one of my faults all my life, and threatens to be even stronger in him'.[6] Albert was struggling to come to terms with the death of his wife, and was suffering great emotional strain when he decided it would be best to proceed with the plans, already discussed with Flora, to send Jack back to England with Warnie. Albert's sincere, if somewhat insensitive, decision to separate the boys from their home is revealed in a letter to Warnie telling him that he loves them both and if he seems harsh it is because he has 'been through the mill' and only wishes to give them the best start in life he can. He adds, 'my one object in living is to start my sons in life as educated Christian gentlemen ... worthy sons of their mother'.[7] The boys did not see it this way though, as Warnie observed, 'with his uncanny flair for making the wrong decision, my father had given us helpless children into the hands of a madman'.[8]

Albert's decision to send the Lewis brothers to a public school in England was motivated by a number of reasons: that they should receive the best

The family on the steps of Little Lea, 1905. Front row (l. to r.): Warnie, Jack, Leonard and Eileen Lewis (cousins); Back row (l. to r.): Agnes Lewis (aunt), two maids, Flora Lewis (mother) and Albert Lewis (father) with the dog Nero.

possible education was a high priority, but class and the desire that his sons should advance on the social ladder were considered equally important. On deciding where to school his children Albert was adamant that the choice was not to be determined by 'good form and football', and had even contemplated sending Warnie to be educated in Germany, adding, 'While I dislike the people from their Braggart Emperor down, even insular prejudice must admit that among European peoples today, they are the doers and thinkers. At all events he will learn the language if he does not drink in anything of their *spirit of thoroughness*.'[9] Flora's concern that her sons should adopt the social graces of such an education can be seen in a letter to Albert where she writes, 'there is much to be said in favour of England; would Armagh be any better than Belfast as regards accent? I doubt it'.[10]

The decision of Albert's brother, William, the first of the Lewises to send a son to an English public school, was a defining moment in the family history. William Lewis was the most socially ambitious of the four Lewis brothers, and his marriage to Wilhelmina Duncanson in 1890 was regarded by the family as a considerable upward social step. He was the least amiable of the brothers, easily depressed and rarely elated, and spent his money on erecting a monument to his exact taste in the form of his house, Moorgate. His brother Richard was the exact opposite, and having no snobbery in his disposition, would emit scornful chuckles at the Moorgate adoption of the practice of 'dressing for dinner'. When Albert and Flora followed William Lewis's example and decided to educate their children in English public schools, they embarked on a course that was to have serious future consequences. Warnie accurately observes that William Lewis's decision to depart from the traditional middle-class family route marked the beginning of the disintegration of the Lewis lineage and reoriented the futures of the next generation in the family. The result of this decision was that class, public school, 'Varsity', Sandhurst, and 'the shop', replaced 'family' as the social unit: this meant that for Jack and Warnie the family had ceased to exist within twenty years.

Warnie clearly views this struggle for social advancement, at the expense of a happy home life, as a major factor in the decline of the Lewis family. That Jack and Warnie never managed to perpetuate the lineage, for whatever reason, is a sad testimony to the accuracy of his observation. Moreover, it is only in the sons of Joseph Lewis, 'the best balanced and most uniformly kindly of the four brothers', that any of the traditional family names perpetuated: 'Norman, Desmond, Leonard, Warren, and Clive, all owe their names either to whims, or to associations derived from the wife's side'.[11] While Albert and Flora were unaware that their social ambitions were part of a process that would lead to the eventual disintegration of the family, they were certainly absorbed by social considerations in seeking a suitable school for their children. They sought advice on schools in Ireland from Albert's trusted advisor and former headmaster at Lurgan College, WT Kirkpatrick, who had previously suggested Trinity College, Dublin as a possibility (presumably this was discounted by Albert and Flora due to the political unrest there). Kirkpatrick wrote again to Albert on the advantages of the public school tone, stating that although it would be marred in Ireland by the ingredient of snobbery, it was certainly preferable to the 'coarseness, vulgarity, and disregard for truth that prevail at the Campbell College'.[12]

From this point on the brothers' fate was sealed and Jack was sent off to join Warnie at Wynyard House school in Watford. Jack's initial reaction to England was one of horror. The train journey from Fleetwood to Euston revealed, 'the miles and miles of featureless land, shutting one in from the sea, imprisoning, suffocating!'[13] The new school was situated in 'Green Hertfordshire' but, 'it was not green to a boy bred in County Down' and he states 'I found myself in a world to which I reacted with immediate hatred'. His distaste was not lessened by the time spent at his new school, which was to last eighteen months. Jack's experience at Wynyard is well documented in *Surprised by Joy*, and the reader will get a general impression of his time there by the title of the chapter 'Concentration Camp' and the pseudonym 'Belsen' for the school in the book.

The most important thing that happened to Jack at Wynyard was that he became an 'effective believer' in the doctrines of Christianity, as distinct from what Warnie had once called 'the dry husks of religion offered by the semi-political church-going of Ulster'.[14] Jack credits this early conversion to the church he was obliged to attend, twice every Sunday, while at Wynyard. This particular church, Saint John's in Watford, was high 'Anglo-Catholic' and Jack's initial reaction was to describe the place as, 'an abominable place of Romish hypocrites, where people cross themselves [and] bow to what they have the vanity to call an altar'.[15] While this attitude would have been in concordance with the sentiments of grandfather Hamilton it was not one that the young boy held with any conviction. Writing many years later he concedes that the experience may have had the very good and opposite effect:

Was I not an Ulster Protestant, and were not these unfamiliar rituals an essential part of the hated English atmosphere? Unconsciously, I suspect, the candles, the incense, the vestments and the hymns sung on our knees, may have had a considerable, and opposite, effect on me. But I do not think that they were the important thing. What really mattered was that I heard the doctrines of Christianity (as distinct from general 'uplift') taught by men who obviously believed them.[16]

This preference for fundamental Christian doctrines as opposed to watered-down Christianity was something Jack would vigorously espouse in later life, and something he shared with his father. On being introduced to the new curate of St Mark's, Belfast, Albert remarked that he had given an excellent sermon on the horror and degradation of war, which gave great offence to many members of the congregation, who liked nothing but 'namby-pamby tosh to be preached to them'.[17] Jack's distaste for the liberalising tendencies of Anglicanism in the 1930s would also come under attack in his first prose work.

If Jack could salvage some positive influences from his time at 'Belsen', Warnie could find little consolation there. He complained to his father that Capron, the headmaster, was making his life a misery by blaming his mistakes on being an 'Irishman' and making fun of him in class with remarks such as, 'Please, we don't want any of your Irish wit here'.[18] Apart from addressing Warnie as 'you great pig, you infernal hog', Capron persisted in these slurs and when Warnie had answered his son back in a minor incident in the school's changing rooms, the headmaster commanded him to 'learn me 50 lines of Virgil, giving cheek to an ex-captain of Eton indeed. Soon we will have Irish home rule here'.[19] This treatment led Warnie to write to his father and beg him to bring them home, adding, 'Now I object to being cursed at by anybody, most of all by an Englishman. I ask you what I asked before, to let us leave, and to let us leave at once, I have stood this sort of thing for three years and I cannot stand it any longer'.[20] Warnie finally escaped from 'Belsen' and began Malvern College, Worcestershire, in the autumn term of 1909. Jack was not so fortunate and had to remain at Wynyard until its collapse in 1910 when Albert, if for no other reason than that the school was permanently closed, relented and brought him home to begin the autumn term at Campbell College, Belfast.

The headmaster of Campbell, James Adams McNeill, was a close friend of

Campbell College, Belfast c 1920.

the Lewis family; in spite of WT Kirkpatrick's misgivings, Albert decided to send Jack and Warnie there: 'Of course, as you say the boys may not be gentlemen, but no big school is entirely composed of gentlemen, and I think English boys are not so honest or gentlemanly as most Irish ones.'[21] The school was about a mile from Little Lea and was named after Henry James Campbell, who left a large estate for the founding of a school 'for the purpose of giving therein a superior liberal Protestant education'. Jack was delighted with his father's decision and as a boarder, he enjoyed the added bonus of being allowed home every Sunday. The most important intellectual event for Jack was his introduction to Matthew Arnold's narrative poem, *Sohrab and Rustum*, by the senior English master, Lewis Alden, known affectionately as 'Octie'.

The only criticism he had of Campbell College, apart from some mild bullying, was that he had no private area to study. Out of school hours were spent either 'evading or conforming to all those inexplicable movements which a crowd exhibits as it thins here and thickens there … One was always "moving on" or "hanging about" … It was very like living permanently in a large railway station'.[22] However, halfway through his first term there Jack fell ill; Albert removed him from school on 15 November 1910, because he had come home that morning with a 'bad cough'. Albert had written a few days earlier that he was worried about his son's 'poor chest – the poorest I think I ever saw in a boy of his years'.[23] This brought to an end his brief spell within the Irish school system. Following a blissful six-week convalescence at home, occupied with reading and drawing, and the Christmas holidays Jack returned to England with Warnie to begin a new school.

Thus, in January 1911, both boys set off to their respective schools. Warnie was already attending Malvern College, and it was decided that Jack should attend the nearby preparatory school, Cherbourg. It was here that Jack lost whatever Christian faith he had. The school matron, Miss Cowie, whom Jack as the 'orphan' adored, was a 'seeker of truth' where spiritual matters were concerned, and as Jack later realised was 'floundering in the mazes of Theosophy, Rosicrucianism, Spiritualism; the whole Anglo-American Occultist tradition'.[24] She, unwittingly and unintentionally, introduced a speculative quality to conversations regarding faith that gradually unravelled Jack's hitherto sincere belief in Christianity, and led him to consider 'the idea that there might be real marvels all about us, that the visible world might be only a curtain to conceal huge realms uncharted by my very simple theology'.[25]

While Jack was contemplating these mysteries in Cherbourg, events of a more monumental nature were occurring in his homeland. In September 1912, Albert had written to Jack informing him of the impromptu general holiday in Belfast and the march of Unionists to the City Hall to sign the Covenant and the attendant bonfires and fireworks that followed. The scenes Albert describes followed the signing of the Ulster Covenant on 28 September 1912, or 'Ulster Day', when 471,414 Ulster Protestant men and women pledged themselves to, 'stand by one another in defending for ourselves and our children our cherished position of equal citizenship in the United Kingdom and in using all means which may be found necessary to defeat the present conspiracy to set up a Home Rule parliament in Ireland'.[26] Jack was obviously not impressed by Albert's emotive description of the event or the sentiments attached to it for we find Albert upbraiding him by return of post for calling the signing of the Covenant 'sconce'.

Albert goes to great lengths in the letter to explain to Jack why he chose not to sign the oath even though he fully supported those who were willing to fight home rule rather than 'be kicked like a pariah dog' from the government of one authority to that of another. His reluctance to sign centres on the conflict of interest between his pledge to uphold the law in his role as police prosecuting solicitor and signing an oath to disobey the law should home rule be passed. Albert's acute sense of honour prevented him from signing a statement stating that he would disobey the law while everyday spending hours prosecuting 'poor, uneducated, half-starved creatures' for failing to do the same. That, he tells his son, would be unworthy of 'a Lewis of Lea'. However, it was not only Albert's honour at stake but Jack and Warnie's future: to sign the Covenant meant that Albert would have to resign his position as police prosecutor and withdraw his sons from school, something he was not prepared to do over an 'evil that may never come to pass'.[27]

This letter reveals a number of things about the relationship between author and recipient. Albert's acute sense of honour and desire to explain thoroughly his motives to his son, coupled with his need for Jack's approval, suggests he was, as he readily admitted, uncomfortable with his failure to sign. It also shows the more practical and paternal concern that his sons should have the best education he could afford. Jack, on the other hand, reveals his growing disillusionment with the political crisis that had dragged on since he penned his own thoughts on the matter in his youthful essay on home rule in 1908. Instead, while Ulster was on the brink of civil war, Jack returned to the stories of talking animals that he had originally begun in Dundela Villas when he was six years old. During the Easter holiday of 1912, he managed to complete a

novel entitled *Boxen: or Scenes from Boxonian City Life*. This novel was in two
volumes, profusely illustrated with intricate colour drawings, and its political
framework is perhaps an imaginative concession to events in his homeland.

While Belfast was experiencing one of the most turbulent periods in its history, Jack was caught up in an overwhelming event of a very different nature.
Strange emotions first encountered in Dundela Villas, when Warnie unveiled
his toy garden and unlocked feelings of 'enormous bliss', now returned with an
intensity that 'flowed together into a single, unendurable sense of desire and
loss, which suddenly became one with the loss of the whole experience ...'[28]
What he discovered was one of the greatest influences on his imagination – the
concept of 'Northernness'. Jack admits an initial 'passion for the Occult': an
interest in fantasy and the supernatural, which surfaced as early as 1914 in letters to Arthur Greeves and seems to have originated in an interest in Norse and
Celtic mythology and the prose romances of William Morris, and later in the
works of George MacDonald, ER Eddison, Lord Dunsany and Mervyn Peake.
Apart from this, his only significant influences at Cherbourg were vanity and
lust. A young schoolmaster named Pogo sparked in Jack the desire for 'glitter,
swagger, distinction, [and] the desire to be in the know' and before long Jack
found himself labouring very hard to make himself into 'a fop, a cad, and a
snob'.[29] The first stirrings of adolescent lust were prompted by the dancing
mistress: while decorating the schoolroom for the winter dance, Jack noted that
she paused, lifted a flag, and sighed ' "I love the smell of bunting" pressed it to
her face – and I was undone'.[30] However, despite these distractions Jack did
very well with his studies and managed to win a classical entrance scholarship
to Malvern College, where he was reunited with Warnie in 1913.

However, he did not share Warnie's enthusiastic account of Malvern and
found life there unbearable. Jack's passion was music and literature, and he had
little interest for the compulsory games that were actively encouraged in the
college. The 'fagging' system that was common in many English public
schools, where the younger boys would act as servants to the older boys, meant
he was frequently picked on and spent his time there exhausted 'both in body
and mind'. This bred in Jack a distrust of cliques or groups that thrived on the
exclusion of others, which he was to satirise in his future works.

However, as with his other schools, there was at least one teacher with whom
he could establish a rapport. His form master, Harry Wakelyn Smith (or Smugy
as the boys called him) was an exceptional teacher who taught Jack the 'right
sensuality of poetry'. Jack recalled that to be in his form was to be ennobled
somewhat, adding, 'Amidst all the banal ambitions and flashy splendour of

school life he stood as a permanent reminder of things more gracious, more humane, larger and cooler'.[31]

The other blessing for Jack was 'the Gurney', or college library, where he could escape the rigours of fagging and it was here he rediscovered the Irish writers that were to have a marked influence on his future writings. Among these were George Bernard Shaw (whom his father, with characteristic flair, had labelled a 'mountebank' though directing him towards the laughs to be had in *John Bull's Other Island*). He also enjoyed James Stephens's *The Crock of Gold*; and the poetry and plays of Yeats, and through him, to Celtic mythology. The works of these authors captivated Jack's imagination and the realities of Malvern were punctuated with periods of ecstasy where Jack could announce 'There were more Leprechauns than fags in that House. I have seen the victories of Cuchulain more often than those of the first eleven. Was Borage the Head of the College? Or was it Conachar MacNessa?'[32] These 'momentary flashes of gold scattered in months of dross' made life at the college bearable, but unfortunately, this same duality was beginning to confound his home life as well.

Jack's growing resentment towards his father began to filter into his writings at this period and is reflected in an unpublished attempt at a short story written around his time at Cherbourg and Malvern. The first attempt at the story, which Warnie calls 'Text A', concerns a character clearly based on Jack's own experiences, asserting a claim to his 'kingdom'. This 'kingdom' is in an old attic room of his father's house and its treasure consists of all the stories, plays, songs, and drawings that the young protagonist has accumulated since early childhood. The father in the story is introduced and when seated, 'silent and unmoving as a Yogi', the tension palpably increases and the character remarks that the silence of the little end room, 'swelled like a bubble till I thought it must instantly burst into some undefined catastrophe'. We learn that the son is fourteen and an only child (his mother had died 'in giving me birth'). The fictional father is in some unspecified 'business', though to the son this merely means that the father leaves the house in the morning and returns in the evening. On his father's return, the youth would have to be seated in the dining room next to the fire, having been 'forbidden' to sit in his 'kingdom' by his father due to his weak chest and persistent colds. The rest of the fragment attempts to articulate and assert his, rather melodramatic, sense of individuality.

These early fragments, while not entirely autobiographical, do contain aspects that echoed the real life relationship between son and father throughout

their life. The palpable sense of relief felt by Jack when the regular holidays
with his father ended and the enforced close contact was lifted, the need to conceal certain facts from his father, and the insistent cross-examination by Albert,
were all frequently expressed in the private correspondence of Jack to his close
friends and brother. The tensions that existed between Jack and his father were
fundamental in shaping these early writings and we see this first version of the
story, written when Jack was still in his teens, with the young author tentatively
exploring his growing uneasiness with his father and attempting to assert his
individuality through fictional defiance. The version of the story which followed this was written when Jack was in his mid-twenties: the story is more
focused, the author considerably older, and the discontent with the fictional
father, who bears more than a passing resemblance to Albert Lewis, is now
more keenly felt with the young man in the story announcing that while he
does not hate his father, he 'hated and feared to be with him'.[33]

The uneasiness the protagonist in both versions of the story feels with the
inquisitive parent mirrors Jack's own relations with Albert, as we shall see later.
Text A also contains an account of adolescent angst that suggests an imaginative amalgamation of his schoolboy experiences at Campbell College. We
learn that the young protagonist made no friends, was in his own words 'a thoroughgoing snob', and having surmounted bullying and general unhappiness,
wins at least toleration from his fellow pupils.

The image of the 'big house' and the 'kingdom' therein as sanctuary and
refuge from the, 'clamour of the boys, the playground, the sordid books', is
subtly evoked. The story also marks the earliest outpourings of Jack's developing romanticism. Following the road up the hill beyond his father's house and
leaving behind 'the fields and works of men', Text A's protagonist passes solitary hours upon the moor smoking cigarettes, reading, writing, and staring
'myself dizzy upon the blue hills or (lying in the heather) upon the tremendous
cliffs and towers of summer cloud, eating out my heart with vague and indistinguishable desires'.[34]

Inevitably, the consequence of being such a 'vain, introspective, prurient,
and romantic' boy was the derision of his peers and this is masterfully and
painfully portrayed in Text A, where he describes himself as a 'dull, slouching,
unattractive boy'. Envying his more popular peers, the 'enforced spectator'
attempts to ingratiate himself by joining in their conversation, perhaps with a
joke 'long meditated' in solitude, only to be jeered, red-faced, into an embarrassed silence. He finds compensation for this treatment in dreams where he is
the 'hero' and people do not 'stare or titter' when he speaks, and if they do he

at least has the courage and strength to hit back. This unfinished story ends with the boy returning home to his father, after a day on the moors, to face his fate. What this fate is we do not know but the imagery used suggests it is not good: it is cold and dark and has been raining all day: 'a cold, slanting rain with a wind that bent the trees and sent their surviving leaves up-sky in showers, wheeling like crows'. The abrupt break in the fragment leaves us wondering just what this confrontation with the father entails and we are aware, in the absence of a sustainable plot, that the story is merely a vehicle for the author to explore his developing romantic imagination and an outlet to vent sublimated hostility towards his father.

That Albert should be the model for the villain of the piece is unfortunate, but this is understandable given the circumstances of Flora's death and Jack's sudden wrench from a happy and secure home. This resentment and uneasiness with his father was something that frequently marred relations between them. For all Albert's anxiety about raising his children, the world he created for Jack after Flora's death was a poor emotional substitute for the solitary and sensitive boy who still regarded his father with fear. Whatever Albert's faults as a parent, nevertheless he loved both his sons, and at considerable expense, supported Jack throughout his long undergraduate years at Oxford. He never wavered in his faith that his son would succeed in securing an academic position suited to his ability and Jack gratefully acknowledged this.

The tension between them was as much due to parental attitudes at the time as to Albert's overpowering personality. What both Warnie and Jack were struggling to extricate themselves from was a situation not uncommon in Ulster life at the turn of the century and is noted by Warnie in his diary for 1967. Rereading a novel by the Irish author, Frank Frankfort Moore, Warnie says:

After tea I began to read *The Ulsterman* and found it as good as ever ... a burning, bitter, but lifelike picture of the Ulster of 1914. The most interesting thing is to find that the dominance, the ceaseless cross-examination, the unawareness that J and I were 'individuals' which we thought was Lewisianism was in fact Ulsterism. True, we were never treated as bad as the Alexander family [in the novel] but in what follows there is enough of our own adolescent grievances to give more than a hint of Leeborough conditions.[35]

In *The Ulsterman*, the younger son, now in his middle twenties, describes living at home on a pittance earned in his father's linen mill:

You know the relative position of father and son in Ulster ... The son is in a worse position than the errand boy. You know the way we have to give an account of ourselves wherever we may go. If I go as far as Belfast for a day, I'm cross-examined as to how I spent every hour. If I get asked out anywhere here I have to ask leave to go. I'm not supposed to make an acquaintance without father's leave ... Well, is it any wonder when we're treated like this, we sons turn out liars and hypocrites? Is it any wonder that we try to get the better of our fathers and show them that we have souls of our own?[36]

This passage contains all the essential elements that prompted Jack's emotional rebellion against Albert. We recognise instantly the similarities between Moore's account of Ulster life and the early story known as Text A. Both contain archetypal characters: younger sons, forced to lie and deceive in order to assert independence, dependent on their father for an income and resentful of it. The driving force in the characters' relationship with their fathers, in both Lewis and Moore's stories, is the need to get the better of them, and only in getting the better of their fathers can the barrier between them be removed and souls be possessed with dignity.

While his enforced exile at school in England damaged his relationship with his father, school holidays at home in Ireland allowed him to enjoy life with

Jack and Warnie with their father and Bill Patterson in 1910.

Warnie and Arthur Greeves. As well as family tennis parties at Glenmachan and expeditions in the Ulster countryside, the brothers were also entertained by family friends, including Bill Patterson, who lived at Garranard about 500 yards south of Little Lea. He was a recognised Strandtown wit, addicted to puns and burlesque, with which he would frequently bombard Albert. He was the member of the family with whom Albert and his sons were most intimate. Warnie describes him as, 'a little, bullet-headed man, clean shaven, and with the wrinkled appearance of a ripe apple'. The brief note that follows was attached to the poem he sent to Albert Lewis: 'With best wishes from the translator. (Don't you wish that he himself was translated?). However, better trans-late than never. Christmas 1914.'

Some recently-discovered additional verses of the Rubaiyat of Omar Khayyam. (The scene of the incidents described is supposed to be a suburb of the city of Baghdad.)

> Wake! For the sun hath scattered into flight
> The shades of darkness with his radiance bright,
> Illumes the hills of SID-NHUM with his glow
> And smites old KAMBHUL-KOLLAJ with his light.

> Before the flare of dawn had wholly died,
> ALI, the sheikh of LITT-LEH loudly cried –
> 'Ho! JAK, when e'en the Meelk-mahn is abroad,
> Why drowsest, lazy loiterer, inside?'

> WI-LI of BAH-NAH long ago hath passed
> On chariot of fire with panting blast.
> E'en JOS-EF, his good sire, will soon pass by,
> Up sluggard! Don thy robes and break thy fast.

> That sprightly Kaliph, BHIL of GAHR-AN-AD
> Hath also gone; his speed is not half bad ...[37]

The astute reader will here recognise the references to Sydenham and Campbell College in Belfast (or Baghdad as the author dubs it). Albert, Jack, and William and Joseph Greeves also make an appearance in the poem. This inspired wit was something the Lewis family greatly enjoyed and even an acceptance note to dine at Little Lea from Bill Patterson would elicit a chuckle:

> Great ALI, since thou nam'st me a glad day
> To feast at thy high board, I'll not say nay.
> Joyful I come, prostrate, with reverence meet.
> When Sheikh's command, Caliphs can but obey.[38]

The Pattersons were a remarkably talented family.[39] According to Warnie, Bill's sister was a skilful watercolour painter; his eldest brother Robert was a singer of professional calibre; and his other brother, Crossley, was an amateur actor of merit. Bill Patterson published a selection of his poems, under the initials, WHF, entitled *Songs of a Port* (McCaw, Stevenson, and Orr, Belfast, 1920). The 'port' being Donaghadee on the east coast of County Down, where he settled with his wife Winnie following the death of his father in 1918. The family also produced for domestic consumption a periodical entitled 'The Pattersonian' which they later had published, for private circulation, as *Selections from the Pattersonian*, (James Cavan, London, 1891). Albert Lewis was obviously impressed since he adopted the idea himself and involved Jack

Jack and Warnie at Glenmachan in summer, 1908.

and Warnie as contributors to 'The Leeborough Review', the manuscript weekly that features Albert's review of Jack's play 'The Jester's Tale'.[40]

Such family productions obviously had a great impact on Jack and Warnie, for many years later they gathered together exactly one hundred of Albert's famous anecdotes in a small hand-written notebook entitled, 'Pudaita Pie'.[41] A typical example of these 'wheezes', as Albert called them, is the story told to him by a Quaker friend of a family party he attended in Ireland where the drink was flowing freely. Realising that the pace of consumption was quite beyond him, he remarked to a member of the family next to him, 'They seem to be a pretty hard-headed lot'. 'Be gor' was the reply, 'there are men at this party that could drink enough to wash a HEARSE!'[42]

William Patterson was courteous and without condescension in his attitude to children and this seems to have endeared him to Jack, with whom he was very friendly. He had a good sense of humour and often told the following story against himself. Accosting a dour Ulster farm labourer digging in a field, he exclaimed: 'My man, in the course of your excavations, I suppose it sometimes happens that you come across some interesting archaeological remains?'. The man stopped digging, rested on his spade, and having favoured his interlocutor with a long stare, resumed his work with the following observation, 'Soul, you're a lad!'[43] This Ulster vernacular phrase, meaning 'you're some boy', meant that the man was bemused and indifferent to Patterson's airs and graces.

Jack and Warnie obviously relished Bill Patterson's madcap humour and evidence of his comic influence can be seen, albeit with a more caustic edge, in their letters to each other where they delight in inventing names for their father. Thus, Albert becomes 'his Excellenz', the 'O. A. B.' (Old Air Balloon) and, slightly more affectionatley, the 'P' daytabird.' This sense of humour certainly helped alleviate the increasing tensions between Jack and his father at this time and was something that would be increasingly relied upon in the coming years.

3 Books and Battle

Two events occurred during the Easter holidays of 1914 that were to have a significant and far-reaching impact on Jack Lewis's life. First, his father, finally realising that Jack's letters from Malvern College begging to be removed were motivated by a genuine unhappiness that refused to abate, made the sensible decision not to return Jack to Malvern the following year. Instead he was to go to Albert's old headmaster from Lurgan College, WT Kirkpatrick, who now worked as a private tutor in Surrey and had successfully 'crammed' Warnie for Sandhurst the previous year. The only condition to this arrangement was that Jack was to return to Malvern to complete his final summer term before joining Kirkpatrick in September of that year.

Second, Jack decided to take up an invitation to visit the son of his father's friend and nearest neighbour, Joseph Greeves, who was convalescing. The boy's name was Arthur Greeves, and the two struck up an immediate friendship that was to last a lifetime. Their first meeting left an indelible impression on Jack:

I found Arthur sitting up in bed. On the table beside him lay a copy of *Myths of the Norsemen*.[1]
'Do *you* like that?' said I.
'Do *you* like that?' said he.
Next moment the book was in our hands, our heads were bent close together, we were pointing, quoting, talking – soon almost shouting – discovering in a torrent of questions that we liked not only the same thing, but the same parts of it and in the same way; that both knew the stab of Joy and that, for both, the arrow was shot from the North … Nothing, I suspect, is more astonishing in any man's life than the discovery that there do exist people very, very like himself.[2]

While the summer holidays of 1914 signalled the eagerly-anticipated end of Jack's schooling at Malvern, it also brought news of an event that was to have direct bearing on Jack's life and those of thousands of his fellow countrymen both in Ireland and Britain. Nearly 100,000 Ulster Protestant men had enrolled in the Ulster Volunteer Force (UVF) with the firm intention to resist home rule by any means necessary. The 'Ulster Crisis' was now coming to a head, and the very real fear that Protestants would have to fight the British Army in order to stay within the United Kingdom was allayed by the news, on 4 August 1914, that Britain had declared war on Germany. The ramifications, for the whole of Ireland and wider Europe, were to be profound.

On 19 September 1914, Jack arrived at Great Bookham, Surrey, to take up residence as a boarder with his future tutor. It was with a certain trepidation that the young man, now approaching his sixteenth year, prepared to meet the almost mythical figure of Kirkpatrick, or 'The Great Knock', eulogised so incessantly by his father, sentiments that were now being echoed by his brother. Warnie, who was living testimony to his skills as a teacher, had gone to Bookham with something of an inferiority complex, partly due to his previous schooling and partly his own indolence; a few weeks of Kirkpatrick's robust teaching methods and kindness towards him soon restored his self-assurance. Kirkpatrick managed, in the space of four months, to transform Warnie from an indifferent scholar to a prize cadet who managed to be placed twenty-first out of 201 successful candidates for entry to the Royal Military Academy at Sandhurst.

Jack's tutor, WT Kirkpatrick, with his wife, outside their home in Great Bookham, Surrey, 1920.

Jack gives a vivid picture of his first meeting with his new tutor, describing him as 'over six feet tall, shabbily dressed (like a gardener I guessed), lean as a rake, and immensely muscular. His wrinkled face seemed to consist entirely of muscles, so far as it was visible; for he wore moustache and side whiskers with a clean-shaven chin like the Emperor Franz Joseph'.[3] William Thompson Kirkpatrick was born at 21 Eliza Street, Belfast, in 1847 and was educated at the Royal Belfast Academical Institution and Queen's College, Belfast. He graduated in 1868 with a first-class honours degree in English, history, and metaphysics and an MA in 1870. He returned to his old school, to take up his first teaching post as assistant master in the English department in 1868 following his first degree, and in the same year entered the Assembly's College, the Presbyterian seminary, in Belfast. He completed the necessary three years in theological studies required for ordination into the Irish Presbyterian Church and was granted his licentiate but was never ordained. When Jack met him he had since declared himself an atheist, but one curious trait from his Presbyterian upbringing survived, as his new pupil wryly noted, 'He spent Sunday, as he spent most of his time on week-days, working in his garden [but] … He always, on Sundays, gardened in a different, and slightly more respectable, suit. An Ulster Scot may come to disbelieve in God, but not to wear his week-day clothes on the Sabbath.'[4]

While Kirkpatrick may have harboured ambitions to become a minister and had gone as far as fulfilling all the necessary criteria, he did not take the next logical step and become ordained. The reasons for this are unknown, but may have had something to do with the stipulation laid down in the rules of his new employers, Lurgan College, which stated that no clergyman, or person in Holy Orders, could have any part in the teaching or the management of the school, and even went as far as to prohibit religious instruction during normal school hours. The college, formerly known as Watt's Endowed School, was established in 1873, following an endowment of £10,000 by Samuel Watt, who had been a prominent local businessman with interests in the brewing and tobacco industries. Kirkpatrick had originally applied for the position of headmaster at the school when it opened but failed to secure the job, and when the post became available again two years later he stressed that while he had trained for the church he was not a minister. This time he was successful and, in time, managed to transform the school's attendance figures from sixteen pupils, when he started, to over sixty within four years. By the late 1880s, Lurgan College enjoyed a reputation as one of the top schools in Ireland.[5]

The depth of gratitude that Jack owed Kirkpatrick is acknowledged in his autobiography, where he devoted an entire chapter to 'The Great Knock'. His excellence as a teacher is corroborated by another past pupil, Robert M Jones, who wrote in the *Royal Belfast Academical Institution Centenary Volume (1810–1910)*:

No boy and no man could be in his company for even a very short period of time without being impressed by the fact that he was in the presence of a man of unusual mental power and grasp, of an overmastering influence on the mind, and of an intellectual honesty and vigour before which pretence and make-believe were dissipated like smoke before a strong wind. None who knew him could be surprised that it was he who subsequently made Lurgan College for many years one of the most remarkable and successful schools in Ireland. He became an almost incomparable teacher, and under him the boys swept to victory over their work and to mastery of their subjects and of themselves. His pistol never missed fire; but he gave you the impression that, if he did, as Goldsmith said of Johnson, you would be knocked down by the butt-end.[6]

The routine adopted at Bookham suited Jack admirably: 'I am going to have the time of my life,'[7] he declared to Arthur Greeves. A normal day would begin with an early rise at half past seven, breakfast at eight o'clock – usually variations of an Ulster fry and 'good Irish soda-bread on the table'– a quick walk in the garden, and then down to work until one o'clock (with a short break for a cup of tea at eleven). After lunch a good walk until four o'clock when he would return for afternoon tea, and then back to his desk and work until seven o'clock when dinner was served. Then talk, letter writing, and reading until bedtime. Jack said of this typical Bookham day:

If I could please myself I would always live as I lived there … Such is my ideal, and such then (almost) was the reality, of 'settled calm, Epicurean life'. It is no doubt for my own good that I have been so generally prevented from leading it, for it is a life almost entirely selfish. Selfish, not self-centred: for in such a life my mind would be directed towards a thousand things, not one of which is myself. The distinction is not unimportant.[8]

Jack thrived under this regime and devoured the Greek and Latin texts Kirkpatrick introduced in his 'purest Ulster' brogue. His method was to read aloud the first twenty or so lines of a text, then translate it into English, hand Jack a lexicon and leave him to get on with it. Any other pupil would have found this muscular approach daunting but not Jack who regarded it as 'red beef and strong beer'. His time with Kirkpatrick was one of the happiest of his life and he made remarkable progress with his studies. It was 'The Great Knock' that Jack credited as supplying him with 'mental muscle'.

In many ways this was the home life he never had, or to be more precise, the home life he should have had. The Bookham environment had a distinctively Ulster tinge to it: among the other boarders there was Terence Forde, who had just arrived from Campbell College to begin his tuition with Kirkpatrick; this added to the sense of an Ulster outpost in deepest Surrey. Jack rarely had any visitors, but he does not seem to have struck up a friendship with his fellow boarder either, and his only contact with the familiar world were the weekly letters from his father and Arthur Greeves. Warnie was serving in France and therefore his letters tended to be less regular. The result of this was that the main influences on Jack at this time, apart from the literature he was so absorbed in, were of an Irish nature, and this goes some way to account for his first real spell of sustained happiness and contentment since his mother's death. Albert would write informing him of the political situation at home and filling him in on the local news while he and Arthur would share their growing enthusiasm for Romantic literature, in particular the poems and plays of Yeats. Meanwhile, Kirkpatrick directed educational operations with the express intention of preparing his pupil for university entrance.

The time spent at Bookham was overshadowed, to a certain extent, by the anticipation he felt at the approach of the holiday periods, when Jack could return to Belfast and reunite with his father, brother, and Arthur Greeves. Jack's new-found happiness at Bookham did not diminish his feelings of displacement and his longing for home as the following letter to Arthur Greeves illustrates:

These last few days! Every little nuisance, every stale or tiresome bit of work, every feeling of that estrangement which I never quite get over in another country, serves as a delightful reminder of how different it will all be soon. Already one's mind dwells upon the sights and sounds and smells of home, the distant murmuring of the 'yards',[9] the broad sweep of the Lough, the noble front of the Cave Hill, and the fragrant little glens and breezy meadows of our *own* hills! And the sea! I cannot bear to live too far away from it. At Belfast whether hidden or in sight, still it dominates the general impression of nature's face, lending its own crisp flavour to the winds and its own subtle magic to horizons, even when they conceal it. A sort of feeling of space, and clean fresh vigour hangs over all in a country by the sea: how different from the stuffiness of Bookham: here the wind – that is to say, the true, brisk, boisterous irresistible wind – never comes.[10]

Queen's Parade Bangor, County Down in the early twentieth century.

The Ireland that Jack experienced and shared with Arthur Greeves was a totally different place to that encountered with his immediate family: the Ireland the two friends shared was a source of inspiration and delight and serves as a romantic backdrop to their literary and imaginative life. If Jack found the proximity of the sea in Belfast invigorating, then the actual experience of Ireland's rugged coastline would have been intoxicating. The Ulster coasts baptised his imagination and allowed him to embrace the concept of 'Northernness' that was to have such a profound influence on his thought and writings.

Jack's relations with his brother had cooled slightly at this time and Arthur Greeves was gradually replacing Warnie as Jack's closest ally. The estrangement with Warnie was prompted by Jack's vociferous condemnation of the Malvern school system that Warnie was so enthusiastic about and the ill-feeling caused by this was allowed to fester during Warnie's prolonged absence at Sandhurst and his later posting to France as an officer with the Royal Army Service Corps. In Warnie's absence, Jack found Arthur Greeves a welcome companion and confidante who shared his enthusiasm for literary discovery and Jack was soon celebrating their friendship in verse:

> That we may mark with wonder and chaste dread
> At hour of noon, when, with our limbs outspread
> Lazily in the whispering grass, we lie
> To gaze out fully in the windy sky –

> Far, far away, and kindly, friend with friend,
> To talk the old, old talk that has no end,
> Roaming – without a name – without a chart –
> The unknown garden of another's heart.[11]

Albert Lewis wrote to Warnie soon after his posting to France: 'If an old chum may give a young chum a little advice. Have little or nothing to do with vin – either ordinaire or particular …'[12] This suspicion was to become only too pertinent in Warnie's case and foreshadowed his intermittent and lifelong struggle with alcoholism. In later years, Warnie would return to Ireland and succumb to the periodic drinking binges that were to afflict him throughout his life. While sober he was an industrious and highly-civilised man, producing seven books on seventeenth and eighteenth-century France[13] as well as editing and typing the eleven volumes that make up *Memoirs of the Lewis Family: 1850–1930*, better known as *The Lewis Papers*. The historian JH Plumb said of him: 'W. H. Lewis knows Versailles better than any man living'[14] and was later astonished to find that Warnie had never been there. John Wain, a fellow member of the Inklings – a group of Christian, male friends who met to talk and read aloud from their compositions – described him as 'the most courteous [man] I have ever met – not with mere politeness, but with a genial, self-forgetful considerateness that was as instinctive to him as breathing'.[15] However, when illness or emotional pressures took hold of him Warnie headed straight, or as straight as he could manage, to Our Lady of Lourdes Hospital at Drogheda. Here, he was always sure – at least in his earlier years – of receiving medical and spiritual attention under the watchful and sympathetic eye of its founder, Mother Mary Martin. Warnie seems to have regarded his visits to Ireland as an opportunity for socialising, invariably winding up in the nearest public house. Jack's view of Ireland on the other hand was essentially imaginative and inspired by the landscape. The difference in the brothers' temperament is alluded to in a letter to Arthur Greeves, where Jack notes: 'The two days and one night were very queer. I found that even with Warnie there the memory of *our* Ireland was stronger than the memory of his and mine … The Ireland I shared with him seemed to be a strictly limited and rather thirsty land: yours was like dewy hills and woods fading into a mist where I felt that one could wander forever.'[16]

The lifelong friendship formed with Arthur Greeves was instrumental in clarifying Jack's ideas about himself and his work. Jack would curb Arthur's tendencies towards self-absorption with a witty riposte that would shake Arthur out of his extravagant melancholy: 'I do not attach much importance to your yearnings for an early grave: not, indeed, because I think, as you suggest, that the wish for death is wrong or even foolish, but because I know that a cold in the head is quite an insufficient cause to provoke such feelings.'[17] The letters from Jack to his friend comprise the greatest collection of letters to one individual in the Lewis canon and the correspondence provides a platform for debate and literary exploration, while at the same time affording Jack the opportunity to dazzle Arthur with his prodigious knowledge. This is not to say that Arthur was merely a foil for Jack's intellectual superiority: Arthur too had a poetic sensibility and an artistic attentiveness to the natural world that rejoiced in, what he termed, the 'Homely'. Arthur would direct his attention from the infinite to the mundane, to another interpretation of beauty, from 'the horizon to ... a hole in the hedge' to 'see nothing more than a farmyard in its mid-morning solitude, and perhaps a grey cat squeezing its way under a barn door, or a bent old woman with a wrinkled motherly face coming back with an empty bucket from the pigsty ...'[18]

Arthur was the youngest of five children. His father, Joseph Malcolmson Greeves, was director of J and T M Greeves Ltd, Flax Spinners, Belfast, founded in partnership by his grandfather and great uncle. The business remained in the family until 1961 when it was amalgamated with Herdman's Ltd, of Sion Mills in County Tyrone. The family lived at Bernagh, just across the road from Little Lea, and were the Lewis family's nearest neighbours. The Lewis brothers offer differing impressions of Arthur's character: Warnie gives a caustic account of Arthur Greeves in *The Lewis Papers*, in which he berates his lack of self-control, self-reliance, and generally pampered upbringing. This view is offset by Jack's more sympathetic account and an accurate picture of Arthur Greeves probably lies somewhere between the two. It should be added that Jack was prompted to write the following account of his friend to supplement Warnie's rather harsh portrait for the purposes of providing biographical details for *The Lewis Papers*. Jack says of him:

Arthur was the youngest son of a doting mother and harsh father, two evils whereof each increased the other. The mother soothed him the more to compensate for the father's harshness, and the father became harsher to counteract the ill effects of the mother's indulgence. Both thus conspired to aggravate a tendency (not rare in human nature) towards self pity ... he taught me to feel with him ... a human affection and a rich aesthetic relish for his antediluvian aunts, his mill-owning uncles, his mother's servants, the postman on our roads, and the cottagers whom we met on our walks. What he called the 'Homely' was the natural food both of his heart and his imagination. A bright hearth seen through an open door as we passed, a train of ducks following a brawny farmer's wife … these were things that never failed to move him, even to an ecstasy, and he never found them incompatible with his admiration for Proust, or Wyndham Lewis, or Picasso … if I had to write his epitaph, I should say of him what I could say of no one else known to me – 'He *despised* nothing'. Contempt – if not the worst, surely the most ludicrously inappropriate of the sins that men commit – was, I believe, unknown to him. He fulfilled the Gospel precept: he 'judged not'.[19]

While Jack was enjoying one of the happiest periods of his life at Bookham, the war in Europe had reached a bloody stalemate on the Western Front. Political concerns in Ulster were defused when the Home Rule Bill, accompanied with an amendment to suspend its operation until the end of the war, became law in September 1914. By January 1916 over 32,000 Ulstermen from the counties of Antrim and Down had enlisted, as the 'farms, mills, workshops and shipyards of Ulster strove to meet the insatiable demands of the Allied war effort. Never had the people been so prosperous and rarely had the island known such domestic peace'.[20] Albert Lewis was, likewise, seized by this patriotic spirit and writing to Warnie in France, informed him that he had joined the Volunteer Corps in Belfast, the object being, in the event of a German invasion, that the citizens would know one end of a rifle from the other and be able to hit something 'smaller than a haystack'. Albert saw his contribution to the war effort as setting an example to the 'picture palace young gentlemen who are sodden with selfishness and cowardice', while conceding that it would be no easy task to 'bring a blush of shame' to those who had still not signed up for active service.[21]

The letters between Jack and Arthur Greeves at this time show little concern for the wider political events surrounding them: their correspondence is filled with a youthful fervour of literary discovery and plans for imaginative collaborations. Jack was also persevering with his ambition to become a poet, and between 1915 and 1917 he completed 52 poems in a notebook, which he called, *The Metrical Meditations of a Cod* ('Cod' meaning 'fool', as in the local expression, 'Amn't I the quare oul' cod'). Jack spent much of the Easter holidays of 1915 composing verse, of which the following extract from *The Hills of Down* is a fairly representative example:

> … Cold, snow pure wells
> Sweet with the spring tide's scent,
> Forsaken fells
> That only I frequent –
> And uplands bare
> Would call for me above,

Were I not there
To roam the hills I love
For I alone
Have loved their loneliness;
None else hath known
Nor seen the goodliness
Of the green hills of Down.
The soft low hills of Down.[22]

Kirkpatrick and Albert Lewis maintained regular contact during this period, to monitor Jack's progress and discuss his proposed future career. Kirkpatrick was in no doubt of Jack's exceptional ability, informing Albert that 'He was born with the literary temperament and we have to face that fact and all it implies.' They eventually agreed, much to Jack's delight, that he should try for a place at Oxford and on 4 December 1916, Jack sat and won a scholarship to University College.

However, Jack was to remain with Kirkpatrick for another three months while he endeavoured to grasp the rudimentary knowledge of mathematics required to pass 'Responsions', a necessary formality for entrance to the university. Jack was invited to begin his first term at Oxford on 26 April 1917 and having failed the Responsions examination twice, he had the good fortune to be exempted due to having joined the Officers' Training Corps as soon as he had arrived at University College. This was indeed fortunate, for, in complete contrast to his mother's aptitude for the subject, he seems to have had a mental block as regards mathematics. But for the university waiving the passing of this examination for those in military service he should, in his own words 'have had to abandon the idea of going to Oxford'.

Albert was divided in his feelings towards Jack's scholarship. On the one hand he was immensely proud of his son's achievement, and on the other he was anxious that his enlisting in the services would endanger him. With one son already serving in France Albert's fears are understandable and he set about, with Kirkpatrick's support, urging Jack to seek an exemption from military service. According to Albert, Jack was eligible, under the Military Service Act, to apply for an exemption on the grounds that he was an Irishman resident in Great Britain for the purpose of his education only.

Jack had written to Arthur Greeves on this subject the year before, mischievously adding, 'By the way take care of that weak heart of yours: it seems pretty sure that CONSCRIPTION is coming to Ireland now. I for one shall be jolly glad to see some relations of mine (and some of yours) made to behave like men at last …'[23] Jack was determined, regardless of parental concern, to do his bit for his country. He would have been bolstered by Warnie's patriotic fervour[24] and that of his fellow Ulstermen, who were enlisting in droves, fearful that the fighting would be over before they reached the Front. Warnie dismissed Albert's argument in favour of getting Jack exempted with the retort, 'What you say about Jack and the other Irishmen of his College is a bit too thick … If being a Nationalist entitles a man to exemption, what is the reward for a Sinn Feiner? An annuity I suppose!'[25]

In his first term at University College in 1917 Jack enlisted, and by June of that year he had joined a cadet battalion and was moved across Oxford to Keble College (which was being used as the officers' training centre). Jack's roommate was a fellow Irishman, Edward Francis Courtenay Moore, or Paddy as he was commonly known, whom he described as 'a good fellow … tho' a little too childish and virtuous for "common nature's daily food" '.[26] Paddy had invited Jack to meet his mother, who had moved from Bristol and taken up residence in Oxford, with her daughter Maureen, to be near her son pending his posting to the Front. Jack took an instant liking to her and spent a week with the Moores, on Paddy's invitation, in August of that year, informing his father that 'I like her immensely and we had a most enjoyable afternoon and evening together'.[27]

Jack (left) with his friend and wartime comrade Paddy Moore (right) in a punt at Oxford, 1917.

Mrs Jane (Janie) King Moore was forty-five at the time she met Jack; she had separated from her husband, Courtenay Edward Moore, in 1907 and moved to Bristol. Her husband, whom she referred to as 'The Beast', was a graduate of Trinity College, Dublin, and the son of Canon Courtenay Moore, Rector of Mitchelstown in County Cork, and worked as a chief engineer for Dublin South-Eastern Railways. She was born in Pomeroy, County Tyrone, the eldest of three daughters and five sons of the Reverend William James Askins. Her father was a curate in Pomeroy before the family moved to County Louth in 1872, where he took up the position of Vicar of Dunany and Dunleer from 1872 to his death in 1895.

It appears that Jack developed an infatuation for Mrs Moore during these visits and soon he was attempting to conceal this relationship with her from his father. On 25 September Jack was gazetted into the 3rd Somerset Light Infantry and given a month's leave prior to being posted. Albert was hurt, and his suspicions aroused when Jack decided to spend the first three weeks of his month's leave with the Moores at their home in Clifton, Bristol, rather than returning immediately to Little Lea. Jack arrived home on 12 October 1917 for the final week of his leave and it seems that relations with his father were somewhat strained, by what Albert perceived as a slight by his son. Jack confided his amorous feelings for Mrs Moore to Arthur Greeves during this stay and then, on arrival back in England, regretting this confession, wrote to Arthur:

Since coming back and meeting a certain person [Mrs Moore] I have begun to realise that it was not at all the right thing for me to tell you so much as I did. I must therefore try to undo my actions as far as possible by asking you to try & forget my various statements & not to refer to the subject. Of course I have perfect trust in you, mon vieux, but still I have no business to go discussing those sort of things with you. So in future that topic must be taboo between us.[28]

Following his week at Little Lea, Jack joined his regiment at Crown Hill, near Plymouth, and on 15 November, after a forty-eight-hour leave, the 3rd Somerset Light Infantry were to proceed to France. Jack had been commissioned as a 2nd Lieutenant with the regiment when, at the last minute, he was suddenly transferred from the 3rd to the 1st division. Before he could get word to his father, he crossed to France on 17 November. Jack had sent a telegram to Albert declaring his imminent departure for France, and requesting him – due to the brevity of the leave – to come to Mrs Moore's to see him off. His father, not understanding the message, wrote back asking for clarification by letter. By the time Albert received Jack's reply, Jack was already in France. On his

Mrs Janie Moore, c 1908.

nineteenth birthday, Jack arrived at the front line trenches. Warnie Lewis, who was serving with the British Expeditionary Force, also in France, was promoted to Captain on the same day.

The most likely reason for this sudden change in regiments is revealed in a letter from Albert Lewis to Colonel James Craig[29] seeking him to exert his influence to get Jack transferred to the artillery. Albert hoped this would prove less dangerous than the infantry, adding that the 3rd Somerset Light Infantry – to which Jack was originally sent – was now in Derry: Albert suggests that the reason for the sudden switch in regiments was due to his being Irish and therefore 'a suspect Sinn Feinner!'[30] Jack refused, having made good friends in his own regiment and not wanting to cut a poor figure in the eyes of his commanding officer, Lieutenant Colonel Majendie, whom he greatly admired. He added that if the artillery had fewer casualties it was because they were smaller in number and were, in fact, under a greater threat from enemy shells, which were more dangerous than rifle fire.

In the end the danger came from another quarter: Jack was taken ill with pyrexia, or 'trench fever', and on 1 February 1918 was admitted to 10th Red Cross Hospital at Le Treport, France, eighteen miles from Dieppe. Albert wrote to Warnie, declaring that it was 'a cause of heartache and bitter tears' that Jack had been laid up in a military hospital. Warnie saw his father's reaction to Jack's illness as evidence of the unreality of the war to those in Ulster not bereaved by it. If a father in England had received such news he would have been overjoyed that his son was removed from immediate danger, and, in Warnie's words, would have thanked God and gone to his day's work 'exulting in the news of the safety of his child'.[31] This sense of unreality was not confined to his father: Warnie recounts a conversation with an able-bodied young shopkeeper in Belfast who, as he was tying up his parcel, summed up the latest war news: 'Well, *we* must just fight it out to the last man and the last bullet!'

War did not lessen Jack's appetite for literature and writing to Arthur from the trenches in France, on New Year's Eve 1917, he enthused over the opening conversation in WB Yeats's play, *The Countess Kathleen*, quoting the first line 'What can have made the grey hen flutter so?' with great delight. This is a recurring feature in Jack Lewis's life: regardless of his private, social, or political circumstances, there was always the impulse to transcend the ordinary and everyday world through literature.

It appears that Jack's new romance with Mrs Moore caused Arthur Greeves some jealousy and anxiety, for we find Jack reassuring him: 'Oh I'd just love to have another of those walks, particularly now in the snow ... Don't think I've lost the taste for all that life. I hope I have gained the new without losing the old and if we were all three – you know my meaning – together somewhere I'm sure we could be very happy, without any clash of interests.'[32] Again, a month later: 'As for the older days of real walks far away in the hills & journeys out of town on top of the tram … Perhaps you don't believe that I want all that again, because other things more important have come in: but after all there are other things besides love in a man's life.'[33] Jack affirms the strength of their friendship and, after Arthur and Mrs Moore had exchanged letters, was overjoyed that 'the two people who matter most to me in the world,' are now in correspondence.

Following his discharge from the military hospital on 28 February, Jack rejoined his battalion at Fampoux before embarking on a four-day tour in the front line of the Battle of Arras in March. He was at the front line again in April, when he was wounded by an English shell on Mount Bernenchon, as the Allies faced the final German attack on the Western Front. Jack received flesh wounds to his hand, leg, and torso, and a piece of shrapnel lodged in his chest. He was moved to the Liverpool Merchants Mobile Hospital at Etaples for immediate treatment before being transferred to Endsleigh Palace Hospital, London, on 25 May, where he remained for a month before being relocated, at his own request, to Ashton Court Hospital, Bristol. While recovering in Endsleigh Hospital, Jack had written to Albert asking him to visit, adding:

You know that I have some difficulty in talking of the greatest things: it is the fault of our generation and of the English schools. But at least you will believe that I was never before so eager to cling to every bit of our old home life and to see you. I know I have often been far from what I should in my relations to you, and have undervalued an affection and a generosity which … an experience of 'other peoples parents' has shown me in a new light. But, please God, I shall do better in the future. Come and see me. I am homesick, that is the long and the short of it.[34]

Albert prevaricated during the summer of 1918, hoping that Jack might be transferred to a hospital in Ireland; he even went as far as trying to get his son into the Ulster Volunteer Force (UVF), hoping that this would secure his transfer. The UVF had been given their own regiment and were renamed the 36th (Ulster) Division in 1914, suffering horrendous losses at the Battle of the Somme in 1916. Jack's frustration with his father's refusal to visit him is apparent in a letter to Albert:

Ever since my last letter to you I have been almost daily expecting to hear from you, and I am rather surprised that neither my answer to your proposal nor my suggestion that you should come over here has met with any reply. Have you not yet decided on a date for coming over? It is four months now since I returned from France, and my friends laughingly suggest that 'my father in Ireland' of whom they hear is a mythical creation like Mrs Harris.[35]

Albert's cautious and methodical nature left him ill-disposed towards any change in his routine and, though suffering from bronchitis, he was well aware how this apparent rebuttal might appear to his son. Confiding his position to Warnie, who was repeatedly enquiring if he had yet visited Jack, Albert writes:

I am sorry – I won't say ashamed – to say that I have not been over to see him yet. Nor do I see a prospect of going soon. I have never been so awkwardly – or at least more awkwardly – placed in the office and Court than I am at the present time. I cannot be certain any morning that my managing man will turn up. If I left home on the spree, the result to my little livelihood would be disastrous. Indeed the worry and overwork is beginning to tell on me. The last holiday I had was my visit to Malvern and some water has flowed under the bridge since then. I have never felt as limp and depressed in my life I think, as I have for the last few weeks. I have no doubt that Jack's thinks me unkind and that I have neglected him. Of course that fear makes me miserable. One night about ten days ago I went to bed worrying about it, and I heard every hour strike from eleven to seven.[36]

His father's misunderstanding which resulted in not arranging to meet him before he was posted to France and the further refusal to visit him in hospital when he was wounded all served to exacerbate the rift between them; it is not without significance that Jack should now come to regard Arthur and Mrs Moore as the two people closest to him rather than his immediate family. Given these circumstances it is not surprising that Jack chose the hospital in Bristol to recuperate, with Mrs Moore living nearby to offer support and comfort during this time. Jack and Mrs Moore were united not only by their growing affection for each other, but by the news that her only son, Paddy, had been killed in action. Replying to Albert's letter of condolence on the bereavement, she writes:

I just lived my life for my son and it is very hard to go on now … They are buried with so many others in that wretched Somme … Of the five boys who came out to us so often at Oxford, Jack is the only one left … I feel that I can never do enough for those that are left. Jack has been so good to me. My poor son asked him to look after me if he did not come back. He possesses for a boy of his age such a wonderful power of understanding and sympathy.[37]

The signing of the Armistice agreement on Monday 11 November 1918 signalled the end of the war and having been demobbed Jack arrived, unexpectedly and to the great delight of his father and brother, for a family reunion at Little Lea on 27 December.

Returning to University College, Oxford, in January 1919, Jack began the honour moderations course in Greek and Latin literature and within a month of his return he was writing proudly to his father with the news that he had just been elected secretary of a literary club in the college called the Martlets. This no doubt evoked fond memories for Albert of his days in the Belmont Literary Society: for all the tensions that existed between son and father at this time they still shared remarkably similar interests and characteristics.

However, Albert did not approve of Jack's relationship with Mrs Moore. Since returning to Oxford, Mrs Moore and her daughter Maureen had taken up residence nearby and an unofficial 'family' was established that was to remain in effect for over thirty years. The nature of the relationship between Jack and Mrs Moore was something that irritated Warnie, 'by its freakishness' and on the one occasion he attempted to bring the matter up with his brother he was told, in no uncertain terms, to mind his own business. Albert too found the situation perplexing, confiding to Warnie that he did not know what to make of the affair save that Mrs Moore was old enough to be Jack's mother and was in 'poor circumstances'. The reasons for Jack's reticence were threefold: he depended on his father for an income, which he was now using to supplement the 'family' income; he was keen to keep this arrangement secret from the university authorities lest his academic career be jeopardised;[38] and he felt guilty about deceiving his father. The result of this deception was that Jack had to maintain an elaborate pretence lest Albert found out he was maintaining three people instead of one.

What is striking at this point is that Jack, coming directly to Oxford from Kirkpatrick's, again establishes firm Irish friendships in England. The 'two people closest to him' at this time were Mrs Moore and Arthur Greeves; we see Jack re-establishing old friendships, and forming new ones, from the Irish diaspora. Among the other Irish friends that were to have an influence on Jack was Theobald Richard Fitzwilliam Butler, whom he first met upon arrival at University College in 1917. Scanning Butler's bookshelf, and finding Keats, Shelley, Wilde, and 'one of the recently executed Sinn Féin poets' among his collection, he warmed to his new acquaintance. Learning that Butler was a frequent visitor to one of Jack's favourite holiday destinations, Portsalon, in County Donegal, further increased his estimation of him and they were soon rhapsodising about their homeland. Jack found he liked the man the more he came to know him and the friendship was christened in a typically Irish fashion when, on one occasion, Butler arrived in Jack's room roaring drunk, declaiming loudly, 'God bless you, God bless you', quoting the sentiments of the Irish poet, Thomas MacDonagh, that he wished he 'were dead, and lying in the woods with the corpses of the great ones of Erin about me ... [concluding] None is unhappier than I, save the great yellow bittern'. Jack was suitably impressed with Butler's ability to preserve his natural civilised character even when paralytic and observed wistfully, 'He used the most beautiful language.' Jack obviously enjoyed his company for we find him and Butler, along with another fellow Ulsterman and former Campbellian, Eric Dodds, celebrating their obtaining 'Firsts' by getting 'royally drunk' (for the first time in Jack's life) and waking up on the floor of his own room the next morning remembering nothing of the night before.

It was during this time at University College that Jack received news that the publisher William Heinemann had accepted his manuscript, previously rejected by Macmillan, of a volume of poems entitled *Spirits in Bondage: A Cycle of Lyrics*, which was written under the pseudonym, Clive Hamilton.[39] The book was published on 20 March 1919 and the common thread throughout is 'that nature is wholly diabolical & malevolent and that God, if he exists, is outside of and in opposition to the cosmic arrangements'.[40] The correspondence between Albert and Warnie, who had both read the book in manuscript, reveal that they thought Jack's declaration of his atheism was unnecessary with Warnie adding, 'that a profession of a Christian belief is as necessary a part of a man's mental make up as a belief in the King, the Regular Army, and the Public Schools'.[41] Albert retained his faith in Jack and, in a comment that does him credit, added that his son would learn in due course that a man had not solved the mysteries of creation at twenty years of age but, if Oxford did not spoil him 'he may write something that men would not willingly let die'.[42] Unfortunately, Albert never survived to learn that his son was to become one the most widely-read authors of this century.

What Albert did not realise was that Jack had been having difficulties with his Christian upbringing since his confirmation. Jack had made his first Holy Communion in St Mark's Church, Dundela on 6 December 1914, without either believing or fully understanding what he was doing. He always felt a sense of guilt over this and in later years he went some way to make amends by offering advice to a god-daughter: 'Don't expect (I mean don't *count on* and don't *demand*) that when you are confirmed, or when you make your first

St Mark's Church of Ireland Church, Dundela in the early twentieth century.

Communion, you will have all the *feelings* you would like to have. You may, of course: but also you may not. But don't worry if you don't get them. They aren't what matter.'[43] These adolescent doubts gradually galvanised into atheism and this persisted throughout Jack's time at Malvern and Great Bookham. That Jack's first published work should explore these doubts was a natural development of his mental and spiritual growth at this time and was the product of many years of contemplation.

Since his time at Great Bookham, Jack had harboured ambitions of being a poet and spent any free moments he had composing verse with the hope that it would one day be published. He maintained this optimistic dedication throughout and we find him writing to Arthur Greeves, while stationed at Keble College as a cadet, declaring: 'I am in a strangely productive mood at present and spend my few moments of my spare time scribbling verse ... I propose to get together all the stuff I have perpetrated and see if any publisher would like to take it. After that if the fates decide to kill me at the front, I shall enjoy a 9 days immortality while friends who know nothing about poetry imagine that I must have been a genius ...'[44]

Spirits in Bondage contains about fourteen poems from the notebook *Metrical Meditations of a Cod*, and the poem 'Death in Battle' that he had managed to get published in John Galsworthy's new periodical, *Reveille*, in February 1919. We now see a new confidence in his writings and a more critical exploration of his Irish background. In the poem 'Irish Nocturne' Jack articulates the growing ambiguity in his feelings for his homeland and in so doing tacitly avows not to fall victim to the same impulses:

> … Oh my heart,
> Looking upon this land, where poets sang,
> Thus with the dreary shroud
> Unwholesome, over it spread,
> And knowing the fog and the cloud
> In her people's heart and head
> Even as it lies forever upon her coasts
> Making them dim and dreary lest her sons should ever arise
> And remember all their boasts;
> For I know that the colourless skies
> And the blurred horizons breed
> Lonely desire and many words and brooding and never a deed.[45]

4 Imagining Ireland

Jack Lewis's friendship with fellow Irishman Theobald Butler had a profound influence on how he viewed his native land. England, and Oxford in particular, afforded Jack the intellectual freedom to explore and reinvent himself in a way he could not in Belfast. The stultifying effect of his visits home are palpable when he confides to Arthur Greeves, 'I found my mind was crumbling into the state which this place always produces: I have gone back six years to be flabby, sensual and unambitious'.[1] The liberating outcome of his friendship with Butler was that he could survey Ireland in a different light, declaring: 'Like all Irish people who meet in England we ended by criticisms on the invincible flippancy and dullness of the Anglo-Saxon race. After all, there is no doubt … that the Irish are the only people: with all their faults I would not gladly live or die among other folk.'[2]

The repressive reality of being an Irishman at home in Belfast compared to being the romantic Irishman in exile in Oxford, produced a highly coloured sense of Irishness: we see Jack dropping many of the prejudices that an upbringing in Ireland invariably produces and avowing that:

I have no patriotic feeling for anything in England, except Oxford for which I would live and die. But as to Ireland you know that none loves the hills of Down (or of Donegal) more than I: and indeed partly from an interest in Yeats and Celtic mythology, partly from a natural repulsion to noisy drum-beating, bullying Orangemen and partly from association with Butler I begin to have a very warm feeling for Ireland in general. I mean the real Ireland of Patsy Macan [sic] etc, not so much our Protestant north. Indeed, if I ever get interested in politics, I shall probably be a nationalist.[3]

The Ireland of Patsy MacCann that Lewis refers to is a combination of fantasy, mythology, realism, symbolism, and meditation, and is depicted in the novel, *The Demi-Gods*, by the Irish writer James Stephens. It is a story of three angels who appear on earth, Donegal to be precise, and accompany the tinker Patsy MacCann and his daughter on a cyclical journey through Connemara, on to

Kerry, before returning north to Donegal. It is an amusing attempt at explaining the ways of man to the gods. Considering the momentous events that occurred in Ireland during this period, it is significant that the warm feelings Jack had for Ireland are for an Ireland of the imagination and not one that reflects the realities of the violent events that led to the formation of the Irish Free State.

The reasons for Jack's ambiguous feelings towards Ulster are partly the result of relations with, and reaction against, his father, and partly the result of his strong sense of morality. Jack viewed his fellow countrymen in the light of Dr Johnson's comment on the Irish: 'They are a fair people; they never speak well of one another.' A former student of Lewis's, Charles Wrong, recalls a conversation with his tutor in which he said something laudatory about Oliver Cromwell; Jack responded immediately: 'I'm afraid I can't agree with you. You see I'm an Irishman. Yes, Northern Irish, but that makes it worse; the offenders you can't forgive are the ones on your own side ... For you to forgive him would be all right, but not for me. "Forgiveness to the injured doth belong".'[4]

This remark goes some way towards explaining Jack's frequently hostile attitude towards what he saw as the 'offenders on [his] own side'; namely, the Orangemen and the Black and Tans, whom he held on a par with 'Hiroshima ... the Gestapo ... [and the] Russian slave camps'.[5] This animosity towards Orangemen was something he retained throughout his life and in 1961 he wrote, 'We have learned from the political sphere that committees of public safety, witch-hunters, Ku Klux Klans, Orangemen, Macarthyites ... can become dangers as great as those they were formed to combat.'[6] Given the tensions between Jack and Albert at this point, the revulsion he felt towards 'noisy drum-beating, bullying Orangemen' is perhaps best understood when one considers that Albert was a proud, though not particularly active, member of a Belfast Loyal Orange Lodge, VII. Jack's romantic vision of Ireland is somewhat tempered when he turns his attention to Ulster: 'The country is very beautiful and if only I could deport the Ulstermen and fill their land with a populace of my own choosing, I should ask for no better place to live in.'[7]

One could argue that Lewis was to do precisely that in his Narnian stories: many aspects of that imaginary world reflect his attachment to the Ulster countryside. Indeed Lewis's innate affinity with the natural world that we see expressed in his letters is characteristic of much Irish writing and reveals a poetic sensibility. The impulse to integrate the Ulster countryside in his work is suggested in a letter to Arthur Greeves. Having just read the novel *Gape Row* by the Belfast novelist, Agnes Romilly White, he commends her on her portrayal of Dundonald life and adds, 'the scenery is quite well described, and it is probably the only chance you or I will have of seeing that landscape described in fiction – except our own of course!'[8]

Lewis's brief flirtation with romantic nationalism occasioned him to announce in 1917, 'If I ever do send my stuff to a publisher, I think I shall try Maunsel, those Dublin people, and so tack myself definitely onto the Irish school.'[9] However, when Lewis published his first volume of poetry, *Spirits in Bondage*, just over a year later, he was less enthusiastic about the Irish literary revival movement. Although he was a great admirer of Yeats – we can see this in his early poetry – he had reservations about expressing himself solely in an Irish context. Seeing the Irish literary revival movement as being, essentially, inferior to the established canon of English literature, Jack was cautious in embracing the ethos expressed by the movement. Attending a meeting of the Martlets, the literary debating club to which he belonged at University College, he remarked, 'a very dull looking youth read a surprisingly good paper on Synge: it has really quite encouraged me to try him again, tho' I feel some grains of prejudice against what I remember of him – perhaps because he has become a cult, which few writers escape now a days'.[10] The reasons for this are at the heart of why Lewis has been considered an English, rather than an Irish, writer and are revealed more fully in the following letter where he cautions Arthur Greeves:

So you are inclining to the New Ireland school are you? I remember you used to laugh at my Irish enthusiasm in the old days when you were still an orthodox Ulsterman. I am glad you begin to think otherwise: a poetry bookshop for Ireland, in Dublin, would be a most praiseworthy undertaking: it might also bring out some monthly journal on Irish literature, containing reviews of contemporary books, articles on classical Gaelic literature and language, and a few poems and sketches. The idea is fascinating: if you could get some big man to take it up …

Here I must indulge my love of preaching by warning you not to get too much bound up in a cult. Between your other penchant[11] … and the Irish school you might get into a sort of little by-way of the intellectual world, off the main track and lose yourself there. Remember that the great minds, Milton, Scott, Mozart and so on, are always sane before all and keep in the broad highway of thought and feel what can be felt by all men, not only a few… It is partly through this feeling that I have not begun by sending my M. S. to Maunsels.[12]

Jack's high ideals were somewhat deflated by the more realistic concerns of getting his first work into print: he admits: 'Of course one sound reason for choosing Maunsel is that they are only a second rate house and therefore more likely to give me some attention.'[13] Having decided to 'keep in the broad high-way of thought', Jack hereafter committed himself to developing his talents within the established English literary tradition. While he absorbed many of the influences of the literary revival movement, he had no real desire to promote the cultural ideals or aspirations associated with it. The reasons for this centre on his aversion to 'eccentricity' as experienced by two very different events: his meetings with Yeats and his time spent nursing a close friend through a severe mental illness.

Jack's two meetings with WB Yeats in Oxford during March 1921 were arranged by a mutual friend, William Force Stead,[14] who mentioned to Yeats Jack's 'double claim to distinction as an Irishman and a poet'. The possibility of meeting one of his literary heroes does not seem to have been overly daunt-ing for Jack for we find him, with youthful insouciance, informing Arthur in October 1919: 'Yeats has taken up his residence in Oxford,[15] and some of us are going to beard the lion in his den one of these days. Perhaps we shall get him to read a paper to the Martlets: perhaps we shall be kicked out. But I think his vanity is sufficient to secure us a good reception if we come with the obvious purpose of worshipping devoutly.'[16]

The first meeting[17] is vividly described by Jack and his impression of Yeats eventually found its way into his first narrative poem. In the preface to his poem *Dymer* (1950 edition), Lewis wrote 'the physical appearance of the Magician in VI, 6–9 owes something to Yeats as I saw him. If he were now alive I would ask his pardon with shame for having repaid his hospitality by such a freedom. It was not done in malice, and the likeness is not, I think, in itself, uncompli-mentary' (page xiv). The bravado with which he earlier informed Arthur Greeves of Yeats's presence in Oxford dissipated when he was actually invited to meet the poet and for the first time he understood 'how it is possible for a man to terrify a room into silence'.[18] The experience is described in detail in a letter to Arthur:

His house is in Broad Street: you go up a long staircase lined with pictures of Blake – Chiefly the 'Book of Job' and the 'Paradise Lost' ones, which thus, en masse, have a somewhat diabolical appearance. The first time I came I found a priest called Father Martindale, his wife and a little man with a grey beard who never spoke, sitting with him. It was a very funny room: the light was supplied by candles, two of them in those 6-ft candlesticks that you see before the altar in some English Churches. There were flame-coloured curtains, a great many pictures, and some strange foreign looking orna-ments that I can't describe. Mrs Yeats lay on a kind of very broad divan, with bright cushions, in the window.

Yeats himself is a very big man – very tall, very fat, and very broad: his face also gives the impression of vast size. There would have been no mistaking which was THE man we had come to see, however many people had been in the room. Grey haired: about sixty years of age: clean shaven: glasses with a thick tape. His voice sounded rather French, I thought, at first, but the Irish shows through after a bit. I have seldom felt less at my ease before anyone than I did before him: I understand the Dr Johnson atmosphere for the first time – it was just like that, you know, we all sitting round, putting in judicious questions while the great man played with some old seals on his watch chain and talked.[19]

The meeting was to influence Jack's thought and work and had a greater bearing on his own personal life than was immediately apparent. Jack had cultivated an interest in the occult since his days at Cherbourg when Miss Cowie, the school matron, had inadvertently loosened the whole framework of his belief by her attempts to disentangle herself from the 'mazes of Theosophy, Rosicrucianism, Spiritualism' and the like. Now he was in the presence of 'a learned and responsible writer' who believed seriously in magic. Jack's attraction towards the occult was a mixture of repulsion and desire and, secure in his atheism at this point, he joked that 'if there had been in the neighbourhood some elder person who dabbled in dirt of the Magical kind (such have a good nose for potential disciples) I might now be a Satanist or a maniac'.[20] The conversation with Yeats added weight and lent legitimacy to the idea that there was a world behind, or around, the material world. Jack's first serious engagement with the spiritual world occurred during the period when he was an avowed atheist, (and a firm believer in materialism) and was prompted by the lure of occultism. That the chief advocate for the preternatural should be one of the most revered Irish poets of his age, and a man whose praises Jack had sung for a number of years, merely served to make the idea more alluring. Of the conversation with Yeats he added:

The subjects of his talk, of course, were the very reverse of Johnsonian: it was all of magic and apparitions. That room and that voice would make you believe anything. He talks very well and not unlike his own printed prose: one sentence came almost directly out of 'Per Amica Silentia Lunae' [1918]. The priest was guardedly sceptical but allowed himself to be argued down. One gets the impression (as I have sometimes got it from others) of a tremendous amount of this sort of thing going on all around us. Yeats 'learnt magic from Bergeson's sister' – 'for a long time I wondered what this dream meant till I came across some Hermetic students in London, who showed me a picture of the same thing I had seen' – 'ah yes – So-and-so: he went in for magic too, but his brain wasn't strong enough and he went mad' – 'at that time I was going through what are known as Lunar meditations etc, etc'. You'll think I'm inventing all this but it's really dead, sober truth. The last two or three years have taught me that all the things we used to like as mere fantasy are held as facts at this moment by lots of people in Europe: perhaps, however you have run across it in town ...[21]

While Arthur was unlikely to find any serious disciples of magic in Belfast, a fellow countryman of Jack's from east Belfast, the dramatist, novelist, biographer, and critic, St John Ervine, had a more intimate knowledge of WB Yeats and his esoteric beliefs. Having worked as manager of the Abbey Theatre in Dublin, which Yeats was involved in setting up, he was well placed to comment on the veracity of some of Yeats's more unorthodox stories. St John Ervine's account of the meeting between Yeats, George Russell, Lennox Robinson, and himself is revealing:

I knew him better as the got-up poet, the dabbler in occultism, the Yogi-hunter, the Celtic Twilighter, the mystic, the fairy chaser, and all the rest of the intellectual clabber in which he delighted. But I knew him also as a shrewd and courageous man who knew exactly how many pence there were in a shilling and intended to get full value for each of them. There was a time when I thought his spookery, as I called it, was pure pretence; but I changed my mind about that when he and George Moore and Lennox Robinson and I dined together one night in Sloane Square during a visit of the Irish Players to the Court Theatre. Yeats was late in arriving. He had been to a spiritualist séance at Wimbledon, and he looked absolutely wrung out when he sat down at the table. No man could affect that appearance. I thought as I looked at him, and I never again doubted that all the stuff he spouted about spirits was sincerely believed. I ought to add that he was not so wrung out that he was unable to make George Moore look like change for three half-pence. Moore who was a frightful gumph of a man, and talked at times like an idiot, was no match for Yeats, who despised him; and when it came to serious argument, Yeats, exhausted as he seemed to be, was far more than his match. Yeats could say more that was worth hearing in five minutes than Moore could say in five years.[22]

This prompted an immediate response from Jack, highlighting an aspect of Irish humour that he was not adverse to employing himself when he wished to evoke a response from an unsuspecting student or colleague. He wrote:

Sir, Mr St. John Ervine of course knew W. B. Yeats better than I, who met him only twice. But on the strength of even two meetings I feel obliged to dissent from Mr Ervine's view that Yeats had no humour ... I count him as one of the funniest *raconteurs* I have ever heard; and in argument (his opponent was no 'gumph', but Fr. Martindale) he had a wonderful – specifically Irish – gift of combining his perfectly serious belief in magic with a mischievous audacity. An Englishman never knew where to have him; and the conclusion of the debate ('Fr. Martindale ye are a sceptic') was excruciating. Yours, etc, C. S. Lewis.[23]

Jack's earlier conversation with Yeats had touched on the link between madness and an unhealthy preoccupation with the occult: this connection was now to touch directly on Jack's life. His only attempt at an 'Ulster' novel was based upon the experience of mental illness, and chiefly concerns Mrs Moore's brother, Dr John Hawkins Askins.[24] The 'Doc', as Jack called him, was the eldest of the three Askins brothers who had all graduated from Trinity College, Dublin. It was their sister Janie who had the task of raising the three brothers (two other children had died young) and her two sisters following the death of their father, Rev William James Askins. It was to her and Jack Lewis that John Askins turned for help in the early months of 1923.

The Doc had moved with his American wife Mary – the 'gaunt she wolf of Washington' – as Jack dubbed her, and their daughter, Peony, to the village of Iffley, just outside Oxford so that he could be near his sister. He and Jack got on well together and Jack concurred with Mrs Moore that 'he is the most unoffending, the gentlest, the most unselfish man imaginable'. The two men, as well as having the common bond of Janie Moore, shared an interest in philosophy and the supernatural and found much common ground for discussion. John Askins's health seems to have suffered following his discharge from the Royal Army Medical Corps in 1917 due to wounds received in battle. Following this he devoted his time to the study of psychology and by January 1923, Jack noted with concern that 'he seems less interested in life than he used to be and can hardly be got to talk outside theosophical philosophy'.[25] This appears to have signalled the first signs of the mental illness that resulted in bouts of depression where Askins would speak of 'the awful depths that one caught sight of underneath one's own mind'[26].

By the end of February 1923, Jack and Mrs Moore agreed to nurse her brother through his increasingly debilitating illness which had now manifested itself as violent fits and the delusion that he was going to hell. Jack added that he 'exaggerated repentance and misery something incredible'. They sent for Mrs Moore's other brother, Rob, who was a medical doctor in Bristol,[27] for help and on his advice they managed to get the Doc admitted to a psychiatric hospital where he eventually died from heart failure on 5 April that year. He was buried at Clevedon on the 10 April and his brother, William Askins,[28] who was

Rector of Kilmore Cathedral, County Cavan, shared the reading of the funeral service.

The effect of this experience on Jack Lewis was profound and radically changed his whole outlook. In a letter to Arthur Greeves he wrote:

We have been through very deep waters. Mrs Moore's brother – the Doc – came here and had a sudden attack of war neurasthenia.[29] He was here for nearly three weeks, and endured awful mental tortures. Anyone who didn't know would have mistaken it for lunacy – we did at first: he had horrible maniacal fits – had to be held down. We were up two whole nights at the beginning and two, three or four times a night afterwards, all the time. You have no idea what it is like. He had the delusion that he was going to Hell. Can you imagine what he went through and what we went through?

Arthur, whatever you do never allow yourself to get a neurosis. You and I are both qualified for it, because we were both afraid of our fathers as children. The Doctor who came to see the poor Doc (a psychoanalyst and neurological specialist) said that every neurotic case went back to the childish fear of the father. But it can be avoided. Keep clear of introspection, of brooding, of spiritualism, of everything eccentric. Keep to work and sanity and open air – to the cheerful & the matter of fact side of things. We hold our mental health by a thread: & nothing is worth risking it for. Above all beware of excessive day dreaming, of seeing yourself in the centre of a drama, of self pity, and, as far as possible, of fears … Isn't it a damned world – and we once thought that we could be happy with books and music![30]

Jack had written to Arthur Greeves as far back as November 1916, when he was still under tuition from Kirkpatrick at Bookham, encouraging him to proceed with his attempt at writing a novel: 'What about taking that magic story Mr Thompson told us, for instance, toning down the supernatural parts a bit & making a Donegal novel of the Brönte type? Or else working that local idea of the Easleys and all. Remember the second attempt will be easier & pleasanter than the first, and the third than the second.'[31]

It appears that Arthur did not take up these suggestions and it was not until sometime between 1924 and 1927 that Jack returned to these ideas. He began fusing them, incorporating his disturbing experiences of nursing the Doc through his illness, into what has become known as his Ulster novel.[32]

In the novel, a young Englishman, Dr Easley, receives an unexpected letter from his cousin, Scrabo, congratulating him on the success of his medical career and urging him to visit his sick aunt in Belfast. The young doctor has never met his Irish relations before and is somewhat apprehensive; his only recollection of Aunt Easley is a childhood memory of, 'the smooth repellent expanse of an ample lap of silk' and a voice that called him 'Laddie'. In the Englishman's childhood, his dying mother had written a 'begging letter' to Aunt Easley, appealing to her to look after him. Scrabo Easley wrote back, replying that due to their financial difficulties they could do no more than send five pounds to help. The years had passed without any further contact, with the young man managing to complete medical school ('with the help of strangers'), enjoying 'breezy, delightful, penniless years as a ship's doctor', before settling down and establishing a practice in Bristol. The novel opens with Dr Easley on a ferry from Liverpool to Belfast, as a result of his cousin's letter.

The opening of the story contains numerous allusions to Jack's life in Belfast and England. The young Dr Easley is based on Mrs Moore's brother, Robert Askins, who also set up a practice in Bristol; cousin Scrabo is named after the hill and monument of the same name in County Down, which had left an indelible impression on Jack's memory ('a picture of the deep stony and brambly valleys on the side of Scrabo, wet and grey as they were one night you and I came down that way. "Jesus, the times this knight and I have had!"'[33] Meanwhile, the trip across the Irish sea aboard the Liverpool to Belfast ferry was a feature of Jack's childhood and adolescence. When we hear that Aunt Easley lives in Wanhope Gardens[34] – considering 'wanhope' is Middle English for 'despair' and Lewis included the 'Isle of Despair' in *The Pilgrim's Regress* – we are left in no doubt as to the author's feelings towards this suburb of Belfast

Scrabo Easley's letter of invitation introduces the young Englishman to Irish politics and clearly echoes the many conversations Jack would have endured at Little Lea. Scrabo rebukes 'the rotten English government' for considering applying conscription to Ireland, adding that it would be poor recompense for the 'sacrifices that Ulster has already made' and leave her open to invasion from the 'Southern's'.

The similarities between fact and fiction recur in Scrabo's lamenting of the financial difficulties in which he finds himself ('I see nothing but ruin staring me in the face. Upon my soul if things get much worse, I shall go out and join you.') This was the kind of statement that Albert frequently employed to stress his precarious financial situation, not realising that he was frightening the life out of the sensitive Jack, who took the warnings of their impending departure to the poorhouse at face value.

Once aboard the ferry, Dr Easley observes that the boat is merely an exten- sion of Belfast. The stewards, the smell, the food, the quantities of it all, 'help

Scrabo Tower near Newtownards, County Down in the early twentieth century.

to convince the newcomer that he is no longer on English soil'. There follows a description of the passengers and their Ulster dialect, which could easily be mistaken for 'low Scotch'. Jack has apparently tempered his distaste towards his fellow countrymen – whom he wished previously to 'deport' – and come to look on them with a guarded admiration:

I cannot describe these Ulstermen better than by saying that they realised perfectly a child's dream of what a 'grown-up' ought to be. Their hands were hairy and massive: their movements and voices were sudden, confident and practical: they moved to an incessant jingling of money, flipping of watch chains and rattling of cuffs. They were the strictest uniform of respectability ... I felt instinctively that I was among good sleepers and hearty eaters.[35]

The reserved young doctor is drawn into conversation with one of his fellow passengers, 'a very plump man with a ragged moustache and a face coloured like raw beef-steak', by the name of Hughie McClinniehan. This man reinforces the sense of despair attached to Aunt Easley's lodgings at Wanhope Gardens when he informs Easley that it is a very wealthy neighbourhood, and 'half of the most substantial people in Belfast live up there', among them the McCreedles, the Watchets (who are in the linen trade), and a Mr Macan of Agnew Towers. The Watchets are an allusion to the small fishing town just outside Devon where Samuel Taylor Coleridge and William Wordsworth stayed after the first day of their walking tour and the germ of the idea for Coleridge's poem *The Ancient Mariner* occurred.[36] Mr Macan is probably a tribute to the central character in James Stephens's novel, *The Demi-Gods*, with which Jack was so enamoured.

Dr Easley's companion berates those 'strong healthy young men dodging the war' in terms that are strikingly similar to those Warnie applied to the Belfast citizens who avoided the draft during the First World War. McClinniehan also complains of the British government's failure to provide help for Ulster in her hour of need, reflecting the political concerns that were articulated so vociferously by Albert Lewis. The social ambition of Jack's mother, Florence Lewis, also surfaces in this scene, when McClinniehan chides the parents who were, 'sending boys from here to schools in England. It doesn't do at all. If I'd had my way I'd have sent my boy to Campbell College or the Institution and I'd have all that money in my pocket and far less trouble into the bargain. His mother wanted him to get the accent you know'. The last line takes us back to Flora's discussion with Albert on whether, 'Armagh would be any better than

Warnie at Glenmachan, on leave from France during the First World War, May 1916.

Belfast [Campbell College] as regards accent? I doubt it'.[37] McClinniehan goes on to make the wry note that some of the people now driving cars once didn't know where their next dinner was coming from and that he remembers Joey Watchet's grandfather 'keeping a wee public house at Ballymacarett'. This was something of a social slur and Jack would have been well aware that Ballymacarett had a long history of impoverishment and where there is abject poverty then social ills inevitably follow. As Sybil Gribbon has noted:

One in fifteen of Ballymacarett's population was estimated to attend church in 1908, and not all those absent were deterred by the want of decent clothing or the halfpenny for collection. At seven o'clock when the afternoon opening of the public houses ended, the fringes of respectable and unrespectable touched briefly, and church goers hurried past the 'drunken men and women cast out by the publicans just at the very hour all are going to worship God'.[38]

This first chapter ends with Dr Easley anxiously pondering his imminent visit to Belfast. It is evident that Jack Lewis has drawn heavily on his Ulster upbringing to inject a sense of realism into the dialogue and set the scene for the drama that is to unfold. It is a strong opening chapter that integrates seamlessly the many autobiographical elements into a coherent and convincing narrative.

The second chapter shifts abruptly to a conversation between Dr Easley and a Rev Bonner. Concerned with Aunt Easley's spiritual well-being and state of health, the Rev Bonner had been talking to her about hell and eternal damnation, and according to Dr Easley, he has driven her to the brink of a nervous breakdown. The central dispute is the conflict between Bonner's conviction that he has a moral duty to inform the sinner of the realities of hell and it is the doctor's duty to look after the physical health of his patient. Dr Easley tries to convince him that if only he would allow her to get 'this infernal business' off her mind then she would be a healthier and happier woman. The doctor undertakes to have her eating properly, sleeping soundly, and 'happy as the day's long' within a few months if only Rev Bonner will leave her alone. He replies that it's not the danger of her dying that he's afraid of but that her soul will suffer eternal damnation.

This second chapter incorporates the mental and physical turmoil that Jack endured while nursing John Askins through madness as well as his own changing and conflicting attitudes towards Christianity. His old atheistic certainty had gone and he articulated the various arguments he would once have rejected out of hand within the fictional framework of the novel. If the devil gets all the best lines in Milton's *Paradise Lost*, then Jack is following his example by putting some of the most passionate speeches into the mouth of the sinister Rev Bonner. The effect of this, while not conforming to conversational niceties, is to allow Bonner to build his argument into a crescendo of rhetoric that leaves the bewildered Englishman temporarily lost for words. Rev Bonner then 'pulled up suddenly as if he had become aware of his own excitement', and the fragment ends abruptly with an argument between the two that centres on whether it is 'madness' to believe in eternal damnation or 'madness' not to.

The unfinished Ulster novel can only be understood in relation to Dr Askins's death and Jack Lewis's changing attitudes towards what he considered dangerous byways of thought: he recorded in his diary during the period he nursed John Askins, 'I at any rate am scared off anything mystical and abnormal and hysterical for a long time to come'.[39] It is ironic that the only 'realistic' or 'modern' novel Lewis ever wrote was set in the familiar world of Belfast but should centre on the dangers inherent in the unknown world. This is not really surprising when we consider that the fantasy element in Jack's literary output was his favoured method of escaping the confining aspects of the everyday world. This was alluded to in a letter to Arthur Greeves where he wrote that he yearned to 'see Co. Down in the snow … one almost expects to see a "march of dwarfs" dashing past! How I long to break away into a world where such things were true: this real, hard, dirty, Monday morning world stifles one'.[40]

His aversion to 'cults', whether literary – he used the term to encompass the Irish Literary Revival movement under the auspices of WB Yeats – or supernatural, was now made explicit. Confiding his fears to Arthur Greeves he warned: 'Safety first, thought I: The beaten track, the approved road, the centre of the road, the lights on. For some months after that nightmare fortnight, the words "ordinary" and "humdrum" summed up every thing that appeared to me most desirable.'[41]

Askins's death marks the fundamental turning point in Jack Lewis's personal and literary life and in the years following this we see him exorcising the allure of the 'ravenous, salt lust for the occult', through his writing. At this point, he was content to recuperate mentally and spiritually and to examine his beliefs. His poem 'In Praise of Solid People', expresses this reflective and self-assessing mood:

> Thank God that there are solid folk
> …Who feel the things that all men feel,
> And think in well-worn grooves of thought,
> Whose honest spirits never reel
> Before man's mystery, overwrought.
>
> … And dusky galleys past me sail,
> Full freighted on a faerie sea;
> I hear the silken merchants hail
> Across the ringing waves to me
>
> – Then suddenly, again the room,
> Familiar books about me piled,
> And I alone amid the gloom,
> By one more mocking dream beguiled.
>
> And still no nearer to the Light,
> And still no further from myself,
> Alone and lost in clinging night
> – (the clock's still ticking on the shelf).

Then do I envy solid folk
Who sit of evenings by the fire,
After their work and doze and smoke,
And are not fretted by desire.[42]

5 A Mind Awake

On 16 July 1923, Jack Lewis received news that he had obtained a first in English, adding to his already impressive achievement of a double first in Classics, and bringing his time at University College to an end. The circumstances under which Jack achieved such distinction were remarkable: the turmoil of John Askins's final illness, his own ill health, the reduced time he had to complete the course, and as always, the relentless pressure of trying to help support his new 'family' on an undergraduate's allowance. When we consider that Jack had been moving around rented accommodation, 'most of them vile', with Mrs Moore and her daughter Maureen since 1919, and listing a total of nine different addresses up to 1922 in his diary, we realise just how far he had come from the comfortable middle-class environment of Little Lea. The financial strain was something that Jack had been unaccustomed to at home and attempts to make a home for his new family under such circumstances left him in 'such a rage against poverty and fear and all the infernal net I seem to be in that I went out and mowed the lawn and cursed all the gods for half an hour…[till] I was tired and sane again'.[1]

The completion of his degrees at University College presented him with the urgent task of securing a job. As no vacancies were forthcoming, he managed to survive by marking examination papers, giving private tuition, and eventually, securing a temporary post as philosophy tutor at his old college while the current holder was on study leave in America. It was not until April 1925 that a fellowship at Magdalen College, Oxford, was announced and Jack found himself competing directly with fellow Ulsterman, John Bryson,[2] for the post. Following the academic interviews the two men were invited to a 'dinner of inspection', as Jack called it, at Magdalen College, hosted by its president, Sir Herbert Warren. The political situation in Ulster threatened to hasten the inevitable collapse of the Empire and was therefore a cause for deep concern to Sir Herbert. The president of Magdalen was one of the first signatories to the declaration in support of the British Covenant appeal along with Lord Rothschild the banker, Sir Edward Elgar, Rudyard Kipling, Lord Milner, and other prominent establishment figures. The appeal was launched in May 1914 with the primary objective to 'paralyse the arm raised against Ulster'. The declaration bluntly stated that:

I _____ of_____ am earnestly convinced that the claim of the Government to carry the Home Rule Bill into law without submitting it to the judgement of the Nation is contrary to the spirit of our Constitution, do hereby solemnly declare that if that Bill is passed I shall hold myself justified in taking or supporting any action that may be effective to prevent it being put into operation, and more particularly to prevent the armed forces of the Crown being used to deprive the people of Ulster of their rights as citizens of the United Kingdom.[3]

Jack's academic ability, war record, Ulster conservative background, and general demeanour obviously made a suitable impression on Sir Herbert Warren, for shortly afterwards he was summoned to Magdalen College and informed that he had been selected for the position. On being told of his son's appointment, Albert Lewis recorded in his diary, 'I went into his room and burst into tears of joy. I knelt down and thanked God with a full heart. My prayers have been heard and answered.'[4]

The fellowship in English put paid to any aspirations Jack had to secure a lectureship in philosophy. In a letter to his father he concedes, 'I have come to think that if I had the mind, I have not the brain and nerves for a life of pure philosophy. A continued search among the abstract roots of things, a perpetual questioning of all that plain men take for granted ... is this the best life for temperaments such as ours? Is it the way of health or even of sanity?'[5] The earlier experience with Dr Askins and Jack's decision to keep to the 'broad highway of thought' all served to convince him that 'having once seen all this "darkness", a darkness full of promise, it is perhaps best to shut the trapdoor and come back to ordinary life: unless you are one of the really great who can see into it a little way – and I was not'.[6]

Now that he had secured financial independence from his father, their relationship lightened somewhat; Albert noted that the fortnight they spent together between 13 September and 1 October 1925 was very pleasant and had 'passed without a cloud'. This period of stability allowed Jack to incorporate some of his turbulent experiences during the last decade into a work that was proving difficult to finish. The work dated back to the Christmas holidays of 1916, when Jack had begun a prose tale called 'Dymer' that was based on an idea that came to him of 'a man who, on some mysterious bride, begets a monster: which monster, as soon as it has killed its father, becomes a god'.[7] The story was to go through many transformations and differing forms, including a version called, 'The Redemption of Ask', before it was finally published as a long narrative poem in 1926

Jack described the writing of *Dymer* as 'a purgation' and in it we see him finally laying to rest many of the fantasies and illusions he had cherished since adolescence. His quarrel with Christianity is also addressed within the poem and there is a definite shift from his previous dismissal of Christianity as merely another myth to an attempt, albeit a vague one, to integrate aspects of the resurrection into the narrative.

The poem is a cautionary tale in which the hero, Dymer, overcomes his self-debilitating obsessions to face his destiny. Jack is echoing Yeats's sentiments, 'We fed the heart on fantasies, The heart's grown brutal from the fare',[8] when he makes Dymer the inspiration and catalyst for the inhabitants of 'The Perfect City' to stage an armed and bloody rebellion against the forces of the state. Writing in the preface to the poem he states:

> For it seemed to me that two opposite forces in man tended equally to revolt. The one criticises and at need defies civilisation because it is not good enough, the other stabs it from below and behind because it is already too good for total baseness to endure. The hero who dethrones a tyrant will therefore be first fêted and afterwards murdered by the rabble who feel a disinterested hatred of order and reason as such ... It will be remembered that, when I wrote, the first horrors of the Russian Revolution were still fresh in everyone's mind; and in my own country, Ulster, we had had opportunities of observing the daemonic character of popular political 'causes'.[9]

The revolt of Bran in Canto IV is portrayed as the inevitable conclusion of anarchy; a direct consequence of Dymer's actions at the start of the poem when he kills his teacher and escapes the totalitarian regime of the Perfect City. Bran soon succumbs to his base instincts and the desire for freedom at the heart of the rebellion merely leads to a different shade of tyranny under Bran, who has become corrupted by power. The theme that runs through much of CS Lewis's thought and writings at this period centres on the need to balance opposing impulses; the need to find the middle ground; the need to keep to the broad highway of thought and not become distracted by wishful thinking, what Jack called 'Christina Dreams' (based on Samuel Butler's heroine, Christina Pontifex, in the novel, *The Way of All Flesh*).

As well as including something of his hatred for public schools and certain aspects of his army experiences in the narrative, Jack draws a portrait of the physical appearance of the Magician in Canto VI, v. 7–8, that is based on his previous meetings with WB Yeats:

It was a mighty man whose beardless face
Beneath grey hair shone out so large and mild
It made a sort of moonlight in the place.
A dreamy desperation, wistful-wild,
showed in his glance and gait: yet like a child,
An Asian emperor's only child, was he
With his grave looks and bright solemnity.

And over him there hung the witching air,
The wilful courtesy, of the days of old,
The graces wherein idleness grows fair;
And somewhat in his sauntering walk he rolled
And toyed about his waist with seals of gold,
Or stood to ponder often in mid-stride,
Tilting his heavy head upon one side.[10]

It is significant that Yeats, who was one of the authors that initially attracted Jack to the supernatural, should play a part in this poetic exorcism of all things eccentric. Jack can now emphatically declare that 'magic or spiritism of any kind was a fantasy and of all the fantasies the worst'.[11] In rejecting the supernatural beliefs of Yeats and what he saw as the associated cultish nature of the literary movement in which Yeats was involved, Jack nevertheless still had a deep attachment to his poetry and, asking pardon for the liberty he has taken in depicting one of his literary heroes, he goes on to pay tribute to his genius:

… a genius so potent that, having first revivified and transmuting that romantic tradition which he found almost on its deathbed (and invented a new kind of blank verse in the process), he could then go on to weather one of the bitterest literary revolutions we have known, embark on a second career, and, as it were with one hand, play most of the moderns off the field at their own game. If there is, as may be thought, a pride verging on insolence in his later work, such pride has never come so near to being excusable.[12]

Jack had discovered that an abnormal interest in the supernatural did not reveal truth but merely a labyrinth of more illusions.

In the preface to the poem, Jack links his meetings with Yeats and the doctrine of magic that he espoused, which 'half fascinated and half repelled' him, with the death of his friend Dr Askins: 'It had happened to me to see a man, and a man whom I loved, sink into screaming mania and finally into death under the influence, as I believed, of spiritualism.'[13] The two are again alluded to in Canto VII of *Dymer* when, having sipped from a drugged cup with the Magician, Dymer lapses into a dream state and experiences visions that at first satisfy and then disgust as he realises that they are not *real*. They lead, as John Askins had discovered to his cost, to delusion:

> And after this night comes another night
> – Night after night until the worst of all.
> And now too even the noonday and the light
> Let through the horrors. Oh, he could recall
> The deep sleep and the dreams that used to fall
> Around him for the asking! But, somehow,
> Something's amiss … sleep comes so rarely now.
>
> … Old Theomagia, Demonology,
> Cabbala, Chemic Magic, Book of the Dead,
> Damning Hermetic rolls that none may see
> Save the already damned – such grubs are bred
> From minds that lose the spirit and seek instead
> For spirits in the dust of dead men's error,
> Buying the joys of dream with dreamland terror.
>
> This lost soul looked them over one and all,
> Now sickening at the heart's root; for he knew
> This night was one of those when he would fall
> And scream alone (such things they made him do)
> And roll upon the floor. The madness grew
> Wild at his breast, but still his brain was clear
> That he could watch the moment coming near.[14]

The end of the poem sees Dymer confronting the 'monster of the night', spawned by lying with one of the immortals – the 'mysterious bride' of Canto II. Casting aside all previous delusions as to what he thought he was, Dymer receives spiritual self-knowledge and prepares to slay the hideous offspring of his false desires. He is quickly slain by the monster, and, in a chapter loaded with Christian symbolism, is transformed into a god with all the attendant spiritual manifestations of spring and the regeneration of nature. The rebirth of Dymer and his ability to face his destiny can only occur through physical sacrifice and the renunciation of past folly. Jack had written in the preface to the poem that just because there is an angel in the last canto one should not assume that 'I had any Christian beliefs when I wrote the poem, any more than … the conclusions of Faust, Part II, means that Goethe was a believer'.[15] This is in one sense strictly true, but the poem articulates a growing awareness of the path to which his spiritual quest is leading.

The Christian connotations and symbolism are employed to illuminate not only his abandonment of previously held vague beliefs and the dangerous consequences to which they can lead, but to signpost the road on which Jack was embarking. The writing of *Dymer* allowed Jack Lewis to put behind him, once and for all, the false illusions of his past:

> … He was whole.
> No veils should hide the truth, no truth should cow
> The dear self-pitying heart. 'I'll babble now
> No longer,' Dymer said. 'I'm broken in. Pack up the dreams and let the
> life begin.'[16]

Following the publication of *Dymer* in September 1926 – again under the pseudonym Clive Hamilton – Jack was still experiencing difficulties in taking the final steps towards accepting Christianity. He lamented the 'unholy muddle' he was in regarding the imagination and the intellect: 'undigested scraps of anthroposophy and psychoanalysis jostling with orthodox realism over a background of good old Kirkian rationalism'.[17] By the start of the following year, after contemplating the doctrine of the imagination in Coleridge and Wordsworth, he asserted, 'That's the real imagination, no bogies, no Karmas, no gurus, no damned psychism there. I have been astray among second rate ideas too long …'[18] However, before Jack was eventually to embrace Christianity another event occurred that was to signal the end of his old life and mark yet another defining moment in his spiritual and personal odyssey.

Albert Lewis was suffering from acute abdominal cramps during the summer months of 1929 and on the advice of Jack's cousin, Joey Lewis,[19] who was a bacteriologist at the Belfast Infirmary, it was decided that he should be sent for X-rays to determine the cause. The tests were inconclusive and an exploratory operation was conducted which revealed what everyone had feared: Albert had cancer. Jack had arrived at Little Lea on 13 August and had been nursing his father, sometimes in terrible agony, throughout this period. The doctors concluded that Albert had every possibility of living for a number of years yet, and

Jack and his father in earlier days at Little Lea, c 1919.

Jack decided to return to Oxford to tackle the ever-increasing backlog of work that had accumulated in his absence. He arrived at Magdalen College on 22 September only to receive a telegram three days later announcing that his father had taken a turn for the worse. He left immediately and arrived in Belfast the next morning only to discover that his father had died at the Nursing Home, 7 Upper Crescent, Belfast, on the afternoon of the previous day.

Even while nursing his father through his illness Jack found himself still drawn between duty and displeasure towards his father. A fortnight before Albert's death he wrote to his friend Owen Barfield: 'I am attending at the almost painless sickbed of one for whom I have little affection and whose society has for many years given me much discomfort and no pleasure ... what in heavens name must it be like to fill the same place at the sickbed, perhaps agonised, of someone really loved, and someone whose loss will be irreparable?'[20] It is ironic that in 1960, at the end of his brief marriage to Joy Davidman, he was to lose a much-loved companion to cancer.

The troubled relationship with his father did not go unnoticed locally. A former curate of St Mark's Dundela, writing recently in the *Church of Ireland Gazette*, recalled 'the sort of chill that previously I had occasionally thought I had seen brought about by a mention of his name' caused by the way in which the Lewis brothers were thought to have treated their father 'with mockery and derision'.[21] However, he was also regarded with some pride in church circles. The widow of Canon GWL Hill, vicar of Glencraig, recounts how a group of clergy were pleased to meet the great man for afternoon tea in the vicarage on one of his visits to County Down.[22]

Warnie Lewis, who was stationed in Shanghai at this time, first heard of his father's death on 27 September when he received a telegram stating: 'Sorry report father died painless twenty-fifth September. Jack.' The previous letters that Jack had sent to his brother detailing the illness did not arrive until a month after his father's death so the news was something of a shock to Warnie. The two brothers were not so overcome with grief that they could not examine their view of Albert in a truthful, yet sympathetic, manner. In a letter to Warnie, a month after the event, Jack writes:

What you say in your letter is v. much what I am finding myself. I always before condemned as sentimentalists and hypocrites the people whose view of the dead was so different from the view they held of the same people living. Now one finds that it is a natural process. Of course, on the spot, one's feelings were in some ways different. I think the mere pity for the poor old chap and for the life he had led really surmounted everything else ... what really got me between wind and water was going into Robinson and Cleaver's[23] to get a black tie and suddenly realising 'You can never put anything down to his account again' ... As time goes on the thing that emerges is that, whatever else he was, he was a terrific *personality*. You remember 'Johnson is dead. Let us go on to the next. There is none. No man can be said to put you in mind of Johnson.' How he filled a room! How hard it was to realise that physically he was not a very big man. Our whole world ... is either direct or indirect testimony to the same effect. Take away from our conversation all that is imitation or parody (sincerest witness in the world) of his, and how little is left.[24]

It is fitting that Jack should pay tribute to his father by aligning him with one of his favourite literary giants: since adolescence Jack had blurred aspects of his father's personality to suit a particular, usually fictional, end. Albert surfaces in Jack's early writings as either the vaguely sinister fictional father in the unfinished fragment known as Text A, or the comic creation of Jack's early play, 'The Jester's Tale', in which he is recreated as 'Poshes', the gloomy individual who, 'under the cloak of pompous disregard for idle jestings conceals an inability to grasp the simplest witticism'. Such was the effect and influence of Albert Lewis that the only way for Jack to escape the tremendously forceful personality of his father was through the writing process.

Robinson & Cleaver's department store in Donegall Square North, seen immediately to the right of Belfast City Hall, c 1930.

It was only in arranging his father's funeral that Jack achieved an understanding of the forces that shaped not only him, but also his whole generation.
During a visit to the undertakers, which Jack described as having 'an insane air
of diabolical farce', for the purposes of choosing a suitable coffin for his father,
Jack found himself bewildered when presented with an array of specimen
coffins: the 'brute' of a salesman slapping one of them like a drum and remarking 'that's a coffin I'm always very fond of'. Albert's brother, William, or
Limpopo as Jack calls him, put an end to this vulgarity when he asked, in his
deepest bass voice, 'What's been used before, huh? There must be some
tradition about the thing. What has the custom been in the family, eh?' Jack
then notes:

And then I suddenly saw, what I'd never seen before: that to them family traditions – the
square sheet, the two thirty dinner, the gigantic overcoat – were what school traditions
and college traditions are, I don't say to me, but to most of our generation. It is so
simple once you know it. How could it be otherwise in those large Victorian families
with their intense vitality, when they had not been to public schools and when the
family was actually the solidest institution they experienced? It puts a great many things
in a more sympathetic light than I ever saw in them before.[25]

The death of Albert Lewis marked a defining moment in his son's life. No
longer was Little Lea viewed as the family home: 'The house has been well suffered in' was Jack's observation and in his poem, 'Leaving Forever the Home
of One's Youth', he lays the ghosts of Leeborough to rest:

> You beneath scraping branches, to the gate,
> At evening, outward bound, have driven the last
> Time of all times; the old disconsolate
> Familiar pang you have felt as in the past.
> Drive on and look not out. Though from each tree
> Grey memories drop the dreams thick-dusted lie
> Beneath; though every place must be
> Raw, new, colonial country till we die.[26]

We have seen how Jack viewed *Dymer* as something of a purgation and the
implications of the story were something that worried him. Having been
reassured by Nevill Coghill[27] that the theme of 'redemption by parricide' in the
poem was neither 'preposterous' nor shocking, Jack managed to eventually
finish the poem.

The Lewis family home, Little Lea, in Dundela, 1919.

Now that his own father was dead, Jack underwent a spiritual rebirth of his own. The tentative steps he was taking towards a full acceptance of Christianity over the last few years were leading him towards what he had been searching for since childhood. Jack Lewis's journey from atheism to Christianity occurred over a number of years and is recorded in depth in his spiritual auto-biography, *Surprised by Joy*. The vague stirrings of what Jack was to later term Joy, first surfaced when Warnie presented him with a toy garden when they were children at Dundela Villas and triggered in him an intense longing for something that he could not define. He only knew that this yearning was 'an unsatisfied desire which is itself more desirable than any other satisfaction' and that anyone who had experienced it would want it again. The importance of this concept of Joy cannot be overestimated: as Jack readily admits, 'in a sense the central story of my life is about nothing else'.[28] The longing for a form in which to express this desire proved elusive. He had attempted to voice the experience in a poem 'Joy', written in 1923:[29]

Today was all unlike another day.
The long waves of my sleep near morning broke
On happier beaches, tumbling lighted spray
Of soft dreams filled with promise. As I woke,
Like a huge bird, Joy with the feathery stroke
Of strange wings brushed me over. Sweeter air
Came never from dawn's heart. The misty smoke
Cooled it upon the hills. It touched the lair
Of each wild thing and woke the wet flowers everywhere.[30]

The writing of *Dymer* had gone some way towards enabling Jack to purge himself of his tendency to indulge in 'wishful thinking', or 'Christina Dreams', but also allowed him to fuse the pagan myth of the dying and reviving god with Christian symbolism. Early in 1926 an event occurred, coinciding with the publication of *Dymer*, that had an alarming effect on Jack: his arguments for rejecting Christianity were being subjected to systematic spiritual attrition, beginning when one of 'the hardest boiled of all atheists I ever knew' (TD ('Harry') Weldon, tutor and college lecturer in the Greats at Magdalen College) sat in his rooms at Magdalen College and announced that the evidence for the historicity of the Gospels was really surprisingly good: 'Rum thing ... All that stuff of Frazer's[31] about the Dying God. Rum thing. It almost looks as if it really happened once. To understand the shattering impact of it, you would need to know the man (who has never since shown any interest in Christianity). If he, the cynic of cynics, the toughest of toughs, were not – as I would still put it – "safe", where could I turn?'[32]

The seventeenth-century Irish philosopher, George Berkeley, also contributed to overcoming Jack's intellectual reticence by providing him with a believable philosophical framework for the existence of God. Berkeley forwarded the bold doctrine of a wholly non-material, theistic universe, whose *esse* was *percipi* – that is 'to be is to be perceived' – and in which human 'spirits' were conceived of as conversing directly with the mind of God. As Harry Bracken has noted:

Berkeley stands committed to a doctrine of substance. He believes that consciousness involves both a perceived (idea) and a perceiver (mind). Neither is reducible to the other. Minds cannot, however, be known via ideas. Ideas are passive, minds are active. We cannot have a passive idea of an active spirit. Knowledge of minds or spirits requires *notions*, a [conceptual] entity by means of which we are said to know spirits and mental acts ... As for God, Berkeley again takes a line from Descartes: some ideas are independent of our wills. But they must depend on some other mind or spirit, i.e. that superior one we call God.[33]

Berkeley's ideas attracted Jack. Having previously immersed himself in the various intellectual arguments while filling in as philosophy tutor at University College, Oxford in 1924, he came to the conclusion:

After all, did Hegel and Bradley and all the rest of them ever do more than add mystifications to the simple, workable, theistic idealism of Berkeley? I thought not. And didn't Berkeley's 'God' do all the same work as the Absolute, with the added advantage that we had at least some notion of what we meant by Him? I thought He did. So I was driven back into something like Berkeleyanism; but Berkeleyanism with a few top-dressings of my own.[34]

In the Trinity term of 1929, Jack overcame his doubts regarding Christianity and 'admitted that God was God'. However, this conversion was to Theism only and Jack was still plagued with doubts about what the Christian doctrine, and in particular the doctrine of redemption, actually *meant*. It was not until October 1931 that he could finally announce to Arthur Greeves, 'I have just passed on from believing in God to definitely believing in Christ – in Christianity'.[35] It was his Christian friends JRR Tolkien and Hugo Dyson who finally convinced him. These two were to later form part of an informal group of friends which included Jack, his brother Warnie, Owen Barfield, Charles Williams, RE Harvard, Lord David Cecil, Nevill Coghill, Hugo Dyson and John Wain. They adopted the name 'the Inklings',[36] and the main thrust of the group was:

... in addition to being friends of C. S. Lewis – perhaps *because* of being friends of C. S. Lewis – were something like a literary movement or at least a reasonably coherent literary school that shared not only Lewis's friendship but in their own ways Lewis's dedication to Christianity. This view holds that the writings of the Inklings constitute a congruous body of literature imbued with an imaginative Christian sensibility especially strong in the area of fantasy and fairy tales ... In other words ... the Inklings ... stand for something real and important that speaks to the issues of literature and belief and their relation to the modern world.[37]

There was no system of membership and composition of the group varied during the 1930s and 1940s. They would usually meet on a Tuesday morning in the Eagle and Child pub in Oxford (better known as 'The Bird and Baby') and on Thursday nights in Lewis's sitting room at Magdalen College (for a detailed account of the group see Humphrey Carpenter's excellent biography, *The Inklings*).

Considering his earlier enthusiastic letter to Arthur Greeves to have been too hasty in affirming his new-found belief, Jack conceded that 'I certainly have moved a *bit*' and confided that he still had difficulties with the phrases he had so often ridiculed in the past, such as 'sacrifice' and 'the blood of the lamb'; phrases he could only interpret in senses that seemed either 'silly or shocking':

Now what Dyson and Tolkien showed me was this: that if I met the idea of sacrifice in a Pagan story I didn't mind it at all: again, that if I met the idea of a God sacrificing himself to himself (cf. the quotation opposite the title page of Dymer)[38] I liked it very much and was mysteriously moved by it: again, that the idea of the dying and reviving god (Balder, Adonis, Bacchus) similarly moved me providing I met it anywhere except in the Gospels. The reason was that in Pagan stories I was prepared to feel the myth as profound and suggestive of meanings beyond my grasp even tho' I could not say in cold prose 'what it meant'.

Now the story of Christ is simply a true myth: a myth working on us in the same way as the others, but with the tremendous difference that *it really happened*: and one must be content to accept it in the same way, remembering that it is God's myth where the others are men's myths: i.e. the Pagan stories are God expressing Himself through the minds of poets, using such images as He found there, while Christianity is God expressing Himself through what we call 'real things'. Therefore it is *true*, not in the sense of being a 'description' of God (that no finite mind could take in) but in the sense of being the way God chooses to (or can) appear to our faculties. The 'doctrines' we get *out of* the true myth are of course *less* true: they are translations into our *concepts* and *ideas* of which God has already expressed in a language more adequate, namely the actual incarnation, crucifixion, and resurrection.[39]

However, the urge 'to call one's soul one's own' was still preventing him from taking the next logical step: 'Every step, I had taken from the Absolute to "Spirit" and from "Spirit" to "God", had been a step towards the more concrete, the more imminent, the more compulsive.'[40] Jack had read GK Chesterton's *The Everlasting Man*, and was plagued by Chesterton's argument that in claiming to be the Son of God, Jesus Christ was either a lunatic, a fraud, or He was speaking the truth. Jack went back to rereading the Gospels and became convinced that the authors were too unimaginative to have created such a story without it having some basis in factual events. Though he had been attending regular Church services since 1929 it was not until two years later, and following his talk with Dyson and Tolkien, that he was finally ready to embrace

Christianity. The final barrier was removed during a decidedly undramatic trip to Whipsnade Zoo in the sidecar of Warnie's motorbike on 28 September 1931. Jack describes this pivotal event in *Surprised by Joy*: 'When we set out I did not believe that Jesus Christ is the Son of God, and when we reached the zoo I did. Yet I had not exactly spent the journey in thought. Nor in great emotion. "Emotional" is perhaps the last word we can apply to some of the most important events. It was more like when a man, after long sleep, still lying motionless in bed, becomes aware that he is awake.'[41]

On Christmas Day 1931 he took the necessary 'leap of faith' required to move from philosophical reasoning to spiritual commitment and made his first communion since childhood in his parish church at Headington Quarry, Oxford.

The imaginative appeal of Christianity as a 'true myth' suited Jack admirably and provided the necessary impetus for him to attempt to tell the central story of his life, the experience of Joy, that had thus far eluded him. Having begun, and then abandoned, a prose version of what he meant by Joy in 1930, he again attempted the same story in verse in the spring of 1932 but to no avail. It was not until a few months later at the home of Arthur Greeves in Belfast (during a two-week holiday in Ireland) that inspiration came and during those two weeks in August he managed to tell the story, not only of Joy, but of his own conversion to Christianity, in prose.

The book was called *The Pilgrim's Regress: An Allegorical Apology for Christianity, Reason and Romanticism*, and, like *Dymer*, sees Jack laying to rest many of the illusions, or 'false Florimels'[42] of his past. The germ of the idea that became *The Pilgrim's Regress* can be traced to the poem 'Our Daily Bread' that appears in Jack's first volume of verse, *Spirits in Bondage*, published in 1919. There is a chilling poetic premonition in the first stanza; a tribute to Jack's friend Arthur Greeves in the second; and a mirroring of the plot of *The Pilgrim's Regress* in the final stanza:

> We need no barbarous words nor solemn spell
> To raise the unknown. It lies before our feet;
> There have been men who sank down into Hell
> In some suburban street,
>
> And some there are that in their daily walks
> Have met archangels fresh from sight of God,
> Or watched how in their beans and cabbage-stalks
> Long files of faerie trod.

Often me too the Living voices call
In many a vulgar and habitual place,
I catch sight of lands beyond the wall,
I see a strange God's face.

And some day this will work upon me so
I shall arise and leave both friends and home
And over many lands a pilgrim go
Through alien woods and foam,

Seeking the last steep edges of the earth
Whence I may leap into that gulf of light
Wherein, before my narrowing Self had birth,
Part of me lived aright.[43]

In the preface to the book Jack attempts to define what he understands by the term 'romantic' literature and proceeds to distinguish at least seven varying definitions of the term. He isolates those that have a particular appeal: his favourite literature being the 'marvellous', provided it does not make part of the believed religion. Thus, 'magicians, ghosts, fairies, witches, dragons, nymphs, and dwarfs are "romantic"; angels, less so. Greek gods are "romantic" in Mr James Stephens or Maurice Hewlett; not so in Homer and Sophocles'.[44] However, these various definitions of 'Romanticism' are inadequate to express what Jack meant by Joy and he admitted to having hastily called it 'romantic' because 'inanimate nature and marvellous literature were among the things that evoked it'. The experience of Joy is nevertheless seen as common, commonly misunderstood, and of great importance, and arising in different people under different stimuli. What unites these disparate experiences is insatiable 'desire', and having followed what he supposed would fulfil these desires for Joy throughout his life – whether it was magic, occultism, romantic literature, or the perfect beloved – Jack found that these were inadequate to it:

On whatever plane you take it, it is not what we were looking for. Lust can be gratified. Another personality can become to us 'our America, our New-Found-Land'. A happy marriage can be achieved. But what has any of the three, to do with that unnameable something, desire for which pierces us like a rapier at the smell of a bonfire, the sound of wild ducks flying overhead, the title of *The Well at the World's End*, the opening lines of *Kubla Khan*, the morning cobwebs in late summer, or the noise of falling waves?[45]

For Jack Lewis these longings converged on one goal, and *The Pilgrim's Regress* is the allegorical story of that journey told through the central 'Everyman' character of John as he works his way from illusion to self-knowledge.

Jack had been working on another book, *The Allegory of Love*, since 1927 and was still in the process of researching when the inspiration for *The Pilgrim's Regress* came. *The Allegory of Love*, published in 1936, charts the history of allegorical love literature from the early Middle Ages to the late sixteenth century and established Jack as a literary historian and critic of some repute in Oxford. Having made a thorough study of how allegory works he was able to draw upon this rich literary history to create a fictional pilgrim's journey that illustrates the dangers lurking off the broad highway of thought. The narrator of the story 'dreams' of John leaving his home in 'Puritania' to embark on a pilgrimage in search of the 'Island' he has glimpsed in a vision. The Island and Joy are inextricably linked: John finds himself in an unfamiliar part of the country near his home and hears a single note of music and a voice from afar beckoning him to 'come'. Looking through the window in the stone wall next to him he sees a green wood full of primroses and he:

… remembered suddenly how he had gone into another wood to pull primroses, as a child, very long ago – so long that even in the moment of remembering the memory still seemed out of reach. While he strained to grasp it, there came to him from beyond the wood a sweetness and a pang so piercing that instantly he forgot his father's house, and his mother, and the fear of the Landlord, and the burden of the rules. All the furniture of his mind was taken away. A moment later he found he was sobbing, and the sun had gone in: and what it was that had happened to him he could not quite remember, nor whether it had happened in this wood, or in the other wood when he was a child. It seemed to him that a mist … had parted for a moment, and through the rift he had seen a calm sea, and in the sea an island, where the smooth turf sloped down unbroken to the bays.[46]

This visionary experience reveals the Island as what he has initially mistaken for the object of his desire, and the subsequent journey becomes an attempt to recapture this. In describing the various dangers that threaten John on his journey, Lewis skilfully enumerates and systematically attacks many of the intellectual, emotional, and political movements of the period. Thus, Freudianism, Modernism, Marxism, Anglo-Catholicism, Humanism, among others, all come under the lash.

Jack had stated in the preface 'the book is concerned solely with Christianity as against unbelief. "Denominational" questions do not come in'.[47] In the closing stages of the book, the pilgrim, with the aid of Mother Kirk [the church], makes the imaginative – and literal – leap into the unknown to become a Christian. He is then told to retrace his steps on the journey that led him to this point and in so doing he now comes to see those ideas that he met on the way as delusions. After confronting and slaying the northern and southern diseases of the soul, in the form of dragons, in scenes that echo and reflect Dymer's struggle, John finds himself back at his parents' house in Puritania that is now empty and ruinous: John, 'his eyes filled with tears', adds, 'I see my father and mother are gone already beyond the brook. I had much I would have said to them. But it is no matter'.[48]

The final chapter sees John crossing the brook by his parents' house to ascend the foothills of the eastern mountains towards the Landlord's Castle, the City of God. The mountains in *The Pilgrim's Regress* are both powerful symbols for the author and an imaginative and concrete link with his past. Jack's solitary pilgrimages upon the Holywood Hills had uncovered the spectacular panorama of the surrounding landscape that fired his imagination and rekindled the first stirrings of Joy. Describing the vista from these hills as a 'different world' he goes on to describe the scenery at length, and, in loving detail, the 'utterly irresistible' feelings it evokes. He had written this in his fifties and age does not seem to have lessened the impact of the experience. Having incorporated the same idea into his early fiction, written in his teens and known as Text A, we again see the dominant image of the Ulster landscape exerting its influence. The young protagonist in the fragment describes the allure of the surrounding Holywood Hills, and the distant Mourne mountains, 'source of all my dreams perhaps even to this day' and questions the ability of the artist to 'recapture that strange longing, that discontent …?'[49]

Having posed the question it is left to the shy and sensitive youth to fulfil the rhetorical demand. Jack's literary writings from this point are nothing less than a series of attempts to recapture this experience of Joy in verse, drama, or prose. The influence of Bunyan on not only the title, but the form and story of *The Pilgrim's Regress* is here made explicit, and marks the genesis of a tale that had preoccupied Jack since his adolescence in Belfast and that was to take over a decade to complete successfully. Like his fictional pilgrim, Jack Lewis was to return to the Christianity of his childhood but, like John, it was to a Christianity that was 'the same yet different': a belief that is utterly transformed and rejuvenated by personal experience.

The significance of the title of the book was not lost on Jack's friend, JRR Tolkien, who noted:

> It was not for some time that I realized that there was more in the title *Pilgrim's Regress* than I had understood (or the author either, maybe). Lewis would regress. He would not re-enter Christianity by a new door, but by the old one: at least in the sense that in taking it up again he would also take up, or reawaken, the prejudices so sedulously planted in boyhood. He would become again a Northern Ireland Protestant.[50]

Tolkien's equating prejudice with Protestantism needs some explanation here. Tolkien was a devout Roman Catholic who appears to have been particularly sensitive to any hint of anti-Catholic bias, whether real or imaginary, partly as a result of the way his mother was treated by her Protestant relatives when she converted to Catholicism. Jack's frequent use of the word 'Papist' in referring to Catholics, however unsettling it may be, should be seen in the light of the age, and the country in which he grew up. The inference that he had a deep-seated animosity towards Catholics simply does not stand up when one turns to his personal correspondence and Christian writings. In the preface to perhaps his greatest work of Christian apologetics, *Mere Christianity*, where he attempts to explain and defend the belief that 'has been common to nearly all Christians at all times', there is an allusion to the denominational difference with Tolkien when Jack says of the Virgin Birth:

> … there is no controversy between Christians which needs to be so delicately touched as this. The Roman Catholic beliefs on that subject are held not only with the ordinary fervour that attaches to all sincere religious belief, but (very naturally) with the peculiar and, as it were, chivalrous sensibility that a man feels when the honour of his mother or his beloved is at stake. It is very difficult so to dissent from them that you will not appear to them a cad as well as a heretic.[51]

Nevertheless, Jack was as quick to react as Tolkien to any supposed slur on his religion. When *The Pilgrim's Regress* was eventually published, Lewis complained to Arthur Greeves:

> … I didn't much like having a book of mine, and specially a religious book, brought out by a Papist publisher … I have been well punished: for Sheed, without any authority from me, has put a blurb on the inside of the jacket which says 'This story begins in Puritania (Mr Lewis was brought up in Ulster)' – thus implying that the book is an attack

Jack's close friend, Arthur Greeves.

on my own country and my own religion. If you ever come across anyone who might be interested, explain as loudly as you can that I was not consulted and that the blurb is a damnable lie told to try and make Dublin riff-raff buy the book.[52]

Lewis had dedicated the book to Arthur Greeves: 'It is yours by every right – written in your house, read to you as it was written, and celebrating (at least in the most important parts) an experience which I have more in common with you than with anyone else.'[53]

While Jack declared that Reason and Romanticism were the paths that brought him back to the Christian religion of his childhood, albeit a more mythical and supernaturally-charged interpretation, it appears that before he could shake off the past and begin his life anew he first had to reconcile himself with his past. *The Pilgrim's Regress* is the book that describes not only the spiritual journey of Jack Lewis but that which also marks the defining and reconciling moment in his attitudes towards his homeland. Following the death of his father, his acceptance of Christianity, and the publication of *The Pilgrim's Regress* we see Jack's Ulster background and influences being absorbed and integrated into a more comprehensive and life-affirming philosophy. He was now able to put aside all his youthful delusions, his hostile feelings towards his father, and his ambivalent attitudes towards his homeland and declare with a new-found moral authority: 'Be sure it is not for nothing that the Landlord has knit our hearts so closely to time and place – to one friend rather than another and one shire more than all the land.'[54] Moreover, this moral authority, first voiced in *The Pilgrim's Regress*, marks the beginning of his career as a Christian 'apologist' and it was a role to which he devoted himself throughout the rest of his life.

It is clear that Jack Lewis underwent a creative and spiritual rebirth at this point and it was only following *The Pilgrim's Regress* that he went on to develop his own distinctive voice. Over the next thirty years, his literary output was phenomenal, and he published more than thirty books: academic works, the Narnian chronicles, Christian apologetics, a space trilogy, a novel, numerous articles and reviews, all flowed from his pen during a sustained period of inspiration. This was a more confident and assured Lewis and this clarity of thought shines through in all of his subsequent writings. By this time he was speaking to all men and not just the few (something he warned Arthur Greeves about years earlier) and while we may give due recognition to the influence of Ireland on Lewis as a writer, he had, as the angels' song at the end of *The Pilgrim's Regress* reveals, now transcended boundaries of birth:

I know not, I,
What the men together say,
How lovers, lovers die
And youth passes away.

Cannot understand
Love that mortal bears
For native, native land
– All lands are theirs.

Why at grave they grieve
For one voice and face,
And not, and not receive
Another in its place.[55]

6 No Rootless Colonist

The question of whether CS Lewis lost his sense of Irishness when he settled in England deserves further examination. Throughout most of his time in Oxford the person closest to him, and with whom he shared his life for thirty years, was an Irishwoman. Whatever Mrs Moore's faults – and she has many critics – she provided Jack with a stable domestic environment in which he managed to complete over twenty books. His next-closest friends were Arthur Greeves and his brother Warnie. Jack's correspondence with Arthur retains the Irish link, and the connection with Belfast in particular, throughout his life. Warnie likewise remained in regular correspondence with his brother during his army service abroad and from December 1932 lived with Jack, Mrs Moore, and her daughter Maureen at their home, The Kilns, in Oxford, until her death in January 1951. The Kilns was thus as 'Irish' a household as Bookham had previously been and the significant feature of CS Lewis's time in England is the Irishness of his domestic habitat. Regardless of how frequently Jack, Janie Moore, and Warnie got on each other's nerves due to this living arrangement there was a bond, beyond their shared investment in the property, that held them together for a considerable period of time. In moving away from his immediate home environment we find Jack working and socialising among fellow countrymen living in England.

Among the Irishmen with whom Jack formed friendships during his time at Oxford, were Mrs Moore's son, Paddy, Theobald Butler, John Bryson, Eric Dodds, and Nevill Henry Kendal Almayer Coghill. Jack first met Nevill Coghill at their tutor's discussion class in University College, Oxford on 2 February 1923, with both sharing the daunting prospect of completing the English School within the year. They took an instant liking to each other and Jack declared him 'an enthusiastic sensible man, without nonsense, and a gentleman, much more attractive than the majority'.[1] The results of the English examination appeared on 16 July 1923 with Jack Lewis and Nevill Coghill being the only two Irishmen, of six candidates, to receive first class honours in the Honour School of English Language and Literature.

Nevill Coghill's friendship was a welcome relief for Jack at this time and was in sharp contrast to the rigours of nursing Dr John Askins, whose first manifestations of mental illness were just beginning to surface. Their second meeting, two days later, confirmed Jack's initial impression of Coghill and he learned that, apart from being born in Cork: 'He had had the appalling experience of being caught by an Irish mob, threatened with lynching, let go, called back again, stood up and pointed at with revolvers, and finally released. He said it was much more terrifying than any war experience. Apropos of my condemnation of Ulster he asked me if I were a Catholic which made me suspect he might be one himself.'[2]

An Ulster background, however loudly one condemns it, requires that you discover 'what foot the other kicks with' and despite being the intellectual Irishman in Oxford, Jack Lewis was still the product of a Belfast environment where such considerations matter. He was wrong in suspicions regarding Coghill's religion. Nevill Coghill was in fact a member of a distinguished Anglo-Irish Protestant family and a nephew of Edith Somerville, who, together with her writing partner and cousin Violet Martin (who used the pseudonym Martin Ross), formed the famous literary partnership of Somerville and Ross and created the comic masterpiece, *Some Experiences of an Irish R. M.*

Jack's growing friendship with Coghill revealed that, apart from being 'the most intelligent and best informed man in the class', Coghill was a Christian and a 'thoroughgoing supernaturalist'. Their conversations on the subject raised a disturbing question in Jack's mind, 'Had something really dropped out of our lives? Was the archaic simply the civilised, and the modern simply the barbaric?'[3] Apart from giving him another nudge towards Christianity, Coghill shared Jack's love of energetic country walks, while joyfully discussing and reciting poetry aloud as they tramped the hills around Oxford.

It was their mischievous sense of humour that led to the following incident at the beginning of 1926. Jack borrowed a volume of TS Eliot's poetry from one of his least favourite pupils, John Betjeman,[4] with the express intention of organising a campaign to embarrass the whole Modernist movement which was gaining popularity among the Oxford intellectual elite. The plan was to submit a parody of modern verse with the hope that it would be mistaken for serious poetry and published as such in either the *Criterion*, which Eliot edited, or the *Dial*. As well as having Coghill on board, Jack enlisted the help of a fellow Magdalen tutor, Frank Hardie, and pupil, Henry Yorke, and together they composed the necessary verse and credited it to the fictitious brother and sister partnership of 'Rollo and Bridget Considine'. Jack noted in his diary:

Bridget is the elder and they are united by an affection so tender as to be almost incestuous. Bridget will presently write a letter to Eliot (if we can get a foothold) telling him about her own and her brother's life. She is incredibly dowdy and about thirty-five. We rolled in laughter as we pictured a tea party where the Considines meet Eliot: Yorke would dress up as Bridget and perhaps bring a baby ... Hardie and Coghill are in it for pure fun, I for burning indignation, Yorke chiefly for love of mischief ... Went to bed, feeling for some reason very nervy and worn out ... perhaps the exhaustion of so much laughter.[5]

Jack then approached William Force Stead, who had introduced him to Yeats in 1921 and whose wife was the sister of Dr John Askins. Stead, a friend of Eliot's (later to baptise him a member of the Anglican Church) was shown one of the parodies and expressed real enthusiasm for it without ever being told that it was meant to ridicule modern poetry. This seems to have ended the jape in this instance and it was not until *The Pilgrim's Regress* in 1933 that Jack would again launch an attack on the Modernist movement. He explained that: 'What I am attacking ... is a set of people who seem to me to be trying to make of Christianity itself one more high-brow, Chelsea, bourgeois-baiting fad. TS Eliot is the single man who sums up everything I am fighting against.'[6] His distaste for the movement did not lessen with age. In a thinly veiled parody on TS Eliot's modern epic *The Wasteland*, in the poem 'A Confession', Jack writes:

> I am so coarse, the things the poets see
> Are obstinately invisible to me.
> For twenty years I've stared my level best
> To see if evening – any evening – would suggest
> A patient etherised upon a table;
> In vain. I simply wasn't able.
> To me each evening looked far more
> Like the departure from a silent, yet crowded shore
> Of a ship whose freight was everything, leaving behind
> Gracefully, finally, without farewells, marooned mankind.[7]

It was Nevill Coghill who helped Jack get his narrative poem, *Dymer*, published by JM Dent and Sons in 1926, after being rejected by Heinemann, who had published his first volume of verse, *Spirits in Bondage*. Following the initial rejection Jack was somewhat taken aback and showed the poem to Coghill for an opinion, who was so impressed with it that he passed it on to a friend who worked for JM Dent and thus the poem eventually made it into print. The two were to remain friends throughout their lives and in a letter many years later Coghill commented on the similarities between Jack and his literary hero, Dr Johnson:

There he was, like the Reynolds portraits (bar the wig) thick-set, full fleshed, deep-voiced, learned, rough, golden-hearted, flattening in dispute, a notable wit, kindly affectioned, with a great circle of friends, some of them men of genius like Tolkien, untidy, virtuous, devoted to a wife untimely lost, liable to give his house over to be occupied, or partly occupied, by people less well endowed than himself, dispenser of secret charities, a Tory and a High Churchman. Could anyone since Dr Johnson be so described except Jack Lewis? And every word true in its fullest sense. When I say 'learned', when I say 'virtuous', I do not mean them in the tomb-stoned sense, where the marble fossilises flattery, but in their most rigorous meanings.[8]

Nevill Coghill was a frequent member of the Inklings, the Oxford literary group with Lewis, Tolkien, and Charles Williams as its nucleus, but his increasing participation in the university dramatic society was to curtail future involvement. However, when he did make it to these gatherings he revelled in one of the group's more eccentric pastimes: the competition to see who could read the longest passage from the novels of the Ulster author, Amanda McKittrick Ros, without being disabled by laughter. This was no mean feat. One of the few who managed this was a former pupil of Jack's, John Wain, whom Warnie records as winning 'an outstanding bet by reading a chapter of *Irene Iddesleigh* without a smile'.[9] For the reader unacquainted with the works of Mrs Ros, the following extract, involving a matrimonial dispute between Irene and Sir John Dunfern, gives something of the flavour of her work:

I was led to believe that your unbounded joy and happiness were never at such a par as when sharing them with me. Was I falsely informed of your ways and worth? Was I duped to ascend the ladder of liberty, the hill of harmony, the tree of triumph and the rock of regard, and while wildly manifesting my act of Ascension, was I to be informed of treading still in the valley of defeat?

Speak! Irene! Wife! Woman! Do not sit in silence and allow the blood that now boils in my veins to ooze through cavities of unrestrained passion and trickle down to drench me with its crimson hue.

Speak, I implore you, for my sake, and act no more the deceitful Duchess of Nante who, when taken to task by the great Napoleon for refusing to dance with him at the State ball, replied, 'You honoured me too much' – acting the hypocrite to his very face. Are you doing likewise?[10]

Mrs Ros gathered many admirers of her books throughout her life. Among those who expressed their admiration was Aldous Huxley,[11] who actively promoted her as 'an Elizabethan out of her time' rather than 'The World's Worst Novelist' as many of the literary critics claimed. Albert Lewis introduced his sons to her work and would regale them with some of her choicest passages on their vacations home. Albert's anticipation is palpable in a letter to Warnie, written in 1915, where he enthusiastically announces the publication of *Poems of Puncture*, by Amanda McKittrick Ros, adding that to the other 'mad eccentricities' of her previous works she had now added 'downright filth'.[12]

Mrs Ros had a highly litigious nature and apart from keeping one solicitor, in her home town of Larne, in continuous employment for at least ten years, she once had six firms of solicitors involved in various lawsuits: three in Larne, two in Belfast, and one in Dublin. Albert Lewis had good cause to be aware of this 'creature', as he called her, for he had previously been on the receiving end of her pen after acting on behalf of a client who was attempting to extract payment from Mrs Ros for services rendered. She wrote to Albert Lewis at his offices in Royal Avenue, Belfast:

Sir,
It has just come to my notice that you had the Tinker-like impertinence to send me the enclosed. Would you be surprised to know that I don't owe Porter one cent? If not, I'm here to inform you. What importation are you, by the by? I thought Belfast already stuffed with such priggish prey. And you demand my damned 2/6 for writing 'THIS' piece of toilet paper. Well I wouldn't give you 2/6 for all the W.C. requisites in Belfast, and solicitors included, mark you – for I hold that all trash emanating from such 'would be's' fit for no other purpose, therefore I return it, inasmuch as you presumably have as much call for it as I, thanks ARFULLY. If such pups as you would mind their own business and not stick your nose into that of a lady's, I consider that you would have quite enough to do, and more than enough. I am quite content to transact my own business without the intervention of such noodles and if I were as near you now as I am to my pen, I'd give your neck a twist you'd probably remember. Whisper – do you owe anything? If so, go and pay it. Just let Mrs. Ros alone, she neither regards you nor all the bloodhounds in Britain one diluted damn.[13]

Albert's reaction to this epistle is unknown.

It is worth mentioning two other more eminent Ulster writers with whom Jack was acquainted, Louis MacNeice and Forrest Reid. During his time as tutor at Magdalen College, Oxford, Jack recorded in his diary:

Bussed back into town and to Betjeman's rooms in St Aldates ... I found myself pitch-forked into a galaxy of super-undergraduates, including Sparrow of the Nonesuch Press. The only others I remember are Harwood ... and an absolutely silent and astonishingly ugly person called MacNeice, of whom Betjeman said afterwards 'he doesn't say much but he is a great poet'. It reminded me of the man in Boswell 'who was always thinking of Locke and Newton'. This silent bard comes from Belfast or rather Carrickfergus. The conversation was chiefly about lace curtains, arts-and-crafts (which they all dislike), china ornaments, silver versus earthen teapots, architecture, and the strange habits of 'Hearties'. The best thing was Betjeman's very curious collection of books.[14]

Jack had much in common with MacNeice had he but known it: both were edu-cated at preparatory and public schools in England; both were brilliant Oxford graduates (MacNeice took a double first in classics and philosophy from Merton College); both were Ulster Protestants from families with strong cleri-cal links (MacNeice's father was the Church of Ireland rector of Carrickfergus); both were united by losing their mothers at an early age; both were directly influenced by Yeats; and both harboured conflicting attitudes towards their native land. MacNeice's view of his birthplace was in stark con-trast to Lewis's sympathetic portrayal of Belfast. In MacNeice's poem, 'Belfast', the city becomes a sinister place to be rejected:

> The hard cold fire of the northerner
> Frozen into his blood from the fire in his basalt
> Glares from behind the mica of his eyes
> And the salt carrion water brings him wealth.
>
> Down there at the end of the melancholy lough
> Against the lurid sky over the stained water
> Where hammers clang murderously on the girders
> Like crucifixes the gantries stand.
>
> ... Over which country of cowled and haunted faces
> The sun goes down with a banging of Orange drums
> While the male kind murders each its woman
> To whose prayer for oblivion answers no Madonna.[15]

MacNeice was appointed to teach Classics at Birmingham University in 1929 by Jack's old friend, Eric Dodds, who was later to act as his literary executor. Coincidentally, MacNeice's most celebrated play for radio shares its title, *The*

Dark Tower, with a story by CS Lewis. There, however, these two Ulstermen part company. MacNeice was an influential figure among the new generation of left-wing English poets that included Jack's old rival for the chair of professor of poetry at Oxford, Cecil Day-Lewis. MacNeice and Day-Lewis, together with Stephen Spender and WH Auden, became the 'MacSpaunday Poets', who focused their poetry on the need for social change. Jack's attitude to such groups and the whole Modernist movement in general is summed up in a letter, written in 1954, informing a friend that he had just been made a professor at Magdalene College, Cambridge: 'I think I shall like Magdalene better than Magdalen. It's a tiny college (a perfect cameo architecturally) and they're all so old fashioned, and pious, and gentle and conservative – unlike this leftist, atheist, cynical, hard-boiled, huge Magdalen. Perhaps from being the fogey and 'old woman' here I shall become the *enfant terrible* there.'[16]

Jack's acquaintance with the Belfast author Forrest Reid seems to have been initiated by their mutual friend, Arthur Greeves. Following a three-year spell at Christ's College, Cambridge, where he was befriended and encouraged to write by the author EM Forster, Forrest Reid returned to Belfast and set up house at 13 Ormiston Crescent, Belfast, not far from Little Lea, where he concentrated on his writing. He wrote fifteen books and numerous articles from here and retained a small circle of close friends. The strength of his friendship with Arthur Greeves was apparent when Reid dedicated his novel *Uncle Stephen* to him in 1931. Two years later Jack would repeat this compliment by dedicating his first prose work, *The Pilgrim's Regress*, to Arthur as a tribute. It is regrettable that Arthur Greeves did not persevere with his literary attempts, considering that he had encouragement and critical support from two of his closest friends who were both established authors. It appears Arthur had set his heart on becoming a 'literary' figure but had yet to surmount the problem of actually writing something. Arthur had consulted Forrest Reid for an opinion on his work and it appears that Reid was none too enthusiastic. He then wrote to Jack in the hope that his old friend would restore his self-confidence and reinforce the idea that he was indeed a 'literary' man. Jack, being a true friend, replied:

So far I have said nothing about Reid's judgement, nor about your going on with the attempt … You must – it is only human nature – be simply starving for some word of *literary* encouragement instead of all this moral encouragement. But don't you also see that I mustn't give it? For as long as you are thinking about *that* [literary fame], still wondering whether Reid is right, you haven't taken the *first step*. Whether you are going to be a writer or not, *in either case*, you must so far die as to getting over putting

The author, Forrest Reid, a portrait by Arthur Greeves.

that question first. The other thing [the work itself] is so very much more important. For be sure, until we learn better, we shall get this kind of suffering again and again.[17]

Having exorcised his own 'Christina Dreams', Jack was not about to see his friend fall into the same trap. Jack had cautioned Arthur four years previously about introducing the 'savage taboo' of incest into his play, 'Trees', arguing that to throw in the subject merely for effect would detract from the play whose 'purpose and interest lie elsewhere'. It appears that the play, like Arthur's other literary attempts, was abandoned before completion. Arthur Greeves's real strength was as an amateur painter. His portrait of Forrest Reid still hangs in Reid's old school, Royal Belfast Academical Institution.

Although Jack had written an article on Forrest Reid for *Time and Tide*[18] in 1946 describing him as 'a neglected artist', on hearing of his death Jack wrote to Arthur, '[he] wasn't a real part of my life, of course, as he was of yours but I liked the man very much – liked him, indeed, better than I could find it easy to explain – something about his voice and face and manner'.[19]

Jack also enjoyed the company of close family in Oxford. Warnie was a more or less permanent member of the household from the end of 1932, and their aunt Lillian Hamilton Suffern also lived nearby at Stile Road. 'Aunt Lily' was his mother's sister and a clever, though somewhat eccentric, woman. Her quarrelsome disposition soon manifested itself following her arrival in Oxford. Jack noted in his diary, 'She has been here for about three days and has snubbed a bookseller in Oxford, written to the local paper, crossed swords with the Vicar's wife, and started a quarrel with her landlord.'[20]

Lily would regale Jack on a variety of subjects, from Shakespeare to religion to philosophy. On being presented with an essay of Lily's for comment, he was pleasantly surprised by its quality, adding 'It is not my line and I hope it is not true, but I must say I thought it great literature.'[21] Lillian was as forceful an exponent of her views as her mother, Mary Warren Hamilton. She was an ardent supporter of the suffragette movement and wrote many letters complaining on the treatment of these women.

Writing in *The Irish Citizen* in 1914, she lambasted the authorities for forcibly feeding a suffragette on hunger strike as a means of punishment. Castigating those men who stood by and would not protest at this treatment she adds, 'They can understand fast enough when it is their own case, and they are proud today of the men who left scores of burnt-out churches in their train in the great reformation which freed us from the Rule of Rome. What men cannot see is that the women's movement is as great a reform as that of Luther, and the spirit behind it is as strong and will manifest itself in the same way when thwarted.'[22]

Jack described her conversation as being 'like an old drawer, full both of rubbish and valuable things, but all thrown together in great disorder,' and goes on to record a visit to her home in 1922:

She is still engaged in her essay, which, starting three years ago as a tract on the then state of woman suffrage, is still unfinished and now embraces a complete philosophy on the significance of heroism and maternal instinct, the nature of matter, the primal One, the value of Christianity, and the purpose of existence ... She told me ectoplasm was done with soap bubbles, that women had no balance and were cruel as doctors, that what I needed for my poetry was a steeping in scientific ideas and terminology, that many prostitutes were extraordinarily purified and Christ like, that Plato was a Bolshevist ... and that Pekinese were not dogs at all but dwarfed lions bred smaller and even smaller specimens by the Chinese through ages innumerable ... I left 'Dymer' with her and got away with some difficulty.[23]

Despite his aunt's peculiar and diverse theories, Jack valued her literary criticism and forthright views. Having left a draft of *Dymer* with her he returned the following week for her verdict. She strongly disapproved of the poem, calling it 'brutal'; adding that he seemed to be deliberately slipshod and wrong in his words, concluding that Jack was 'positively like Bill Patterson'. Although Jack often found her arrogant self-assuredness trying – '... the Holy Ghost discusses all his plans with her and she was on the committee that arranged creation'[24] – he was genuinely fond of her. She remained the closest link to his own mother and added a touch of the unexpected to Jack's circle of Irish friends and family in Oxford.

As well as the influence of Irish people in his Oxford life, Lewis retained a physical link by frequent contact with Ireland. CS Lewis's closeness to his homeland is nowhere more evident than in his affinity with, and attentiveness to, the natural world. A childhood spent within sight of the mountains of Antrim and Down was among his most vivid memories and these 'unattainable blue hills' helped to encourage his romantic bent. Jack describes his main haunt as the Holywood Hills – 'the irregular polygon you would have described if you drew a line from Stormont to Comber, from Comber to Newtownards, from Newtownards to Scrabo, from Scrabo to Craigantlet, from Craigantlet to Holywood, and thence through Knocknagon[n]ey back to Stormont'.[25] In *Surprised by Joy*, Belfast and the surrounding Ulster landscape is depicted with

The Crawfordsburn Inn, County Down, c 1950, where Lewis stayed when visiting Arthur Greeves and also while on honeymoon.

poetic clarity and rigorous attention to detail as Jack invites the reader to share in this glorification of place:

Stand at the north-eastern extremity where the slopes go steeply down to Holywood. Beneath you is the whole expanse of the Lough. The Antrim coast twists sharply to the north and out of sight; green, and humble in comparison, Down curves away southward. Between the two the Lough merges into the sea, and if you look carefully on a good day you can even see Scotland, phantom-like on the horizon. Now come further to the south and west. Take your stand at the isolated cottage which is visible from my father's house and overlooks our whole suburb, and which everyone calls The Shepherd's Hut, though we are not really a shepherd country. You are still looking down on the Lough ... Your horizon from here is the Antrim Mountains, probably a uniform mass of greyish blue, though if it is a sunny day you may just trace on the Cave Hill the distinction between the green slopes that climb two thirds of the way to the summit and the cliff wall that perpendicularly accomplishes the rest. That is one beauty; and here where you stand is another, quite different and even more dearly loved – sunlight and grass and dew, crowing cocks and gaggling ducks. In between them, on the flat floor of the Valley at your feet, a forest of factory chimneys, gantries, and giant cranes rising out of a welter of mist, lies Belfast. Noises come up from it continually, whining and screeching of trams, clatter of horse traffic on uneven streets, and dominating all else, the continual throb and

The Harland & Wolff shipyard, seen from Victoria Park, Sydenham, in east Belfast. Early twentieth century.

stammer of the great shipyards. And because we have heard this all our lives it does not, for us, violate the peace of the hill-top; rather, it emphasises it, enriches the contrast, sharpens the dualism ... Now step a little way – only two fields and across a lane up to the top of the bank on the far side – and you will see, looking south with a little east in it, a different world. And having seen it blame me if you can for being a romantic. For here is the thing itself, utterly irresistible, the way to the world's end, the land of longing, the breaking and blessing of hearts. You are looking across what may be called, in a certain sense the plain of Down, and seeing beyond it the Mourne Mountains.[26]

The 'turbulent democracy of little hills' that is the County Down landscape exerted an irresistible heightening of awareness on Jack: they combined the vague longings of his childhood experience of Joy with a physical presence that dominated the perceived world. The Irish landscape also provided a concrete link with his past and an endless source of imaginative inspiration. Having consciously cultivated the habit of being 'a mere sponge to sense impressions',[27] we see him absorbing these influences and transfiguring the reality around him to help create the imaginary worlds of his supernatural fiction. The absorption in, and variety of, the natural world reveals to him just 'how broad-minded the infinite is'[28] and opened up the possibilities of finding the marvellous hidden in the mundane. Thus he told Arthur Greeves:

After tea I went out, thro' old Headington and over the fields towards Forest Hill ... The evening was wildly cold. Mark what I say: not *intensely* cold, but wildly: i.e. tho there was little movement in the air the cold gave the feeling of *wildness* to the world – a raging silence. I walked out over the big fields and behind me there was the flaming orange that you often get at frosty sunset, but only a thin strip, and above that – green: then above that silver: above my head – at the zenith – stars: before me the moon, at present dead & lightless tho' white, a little above the horizon. I walked faster and faster as one does in sympathy with such 'wildness' until – when I had come out of the big fields and was going up among the pines to where you and I sat, rather a funny experience happened. I had not noticed any change in the light: moon rising and sun setting had so evenly divided the sky that there was no break, and I still attributed the light in which I walked to the sunset behind me. Imagine then what it was like when with a quiet shock I saw my shadow *following* me over the turf and thus *in the shadow* first perceived how bright the moonlight must be. I'm afraid I can hardly express it in a letter. At any rate the whole walk was wonderful, and that bit in particular ghostly – ghostly in the good sense, not in the spookikal.[29]

The senses are here fully engaged. His poetic sensibility and attentiveness to his surroundings illuminate Lewis's 'nature writings'. These nature writings are scattered throughout the letters and diary entries and originate from what the Romantic poets would call the spontaneous overflow of powerfully-felt emotions. We have seen earlier how the young Lewis would 'stare himself dizzy upon the blue hills', eating his heart out with 'vague and indistinguishable desires'. From an early age he was struggling to capture these romantic impulses and sensations in prose and verse, with some measure of success. This imaginative apprenticeship was served chiefly among the Holywood Hills and the surrounding countryside, establishing an aesthetic link with Ulster that remained throughout his life.

The Belfast Hotel, Holywood, County Down where Jack and Warnie would stop for a drink after walking through the Holywood Hills.

The frequent walking tours that Jack undertook with his brother (usually in January) and other friends at Oxford (for a week in the spring), were an important part of his year. They would set off on a planned route and travel on foot, making stops at village inns on the way for refreshments and lodgings, and usually managed to cover up to twenty miles a day on their journey. They would indulge in imaginative speculation, conversation, foolery, and an appreciation of the variety of the English countryside. The essence and attraction of the walking tour lies in its simplicity: one has only to consider the fundamentals; food, shelter, and reaching the next destination on the map. For Jack, the joy felt after a day's walking, perhaps in extreme weather, and the relief of spying the lights of a village in the distance where he would spend the night, 'fixes itself in your mind – for enjoyment ten, twenty, or thirty years hence – as a place of impossible peace and dreaminess'.

The experiences of the walking tours also supplied a rich stock of images that embellished CS Lewis's fiction. In the first book of his science fiction trilogy, *Out of the Silent Planet*, the story opens with Dr Elwin Ransom, a middle-aged philologist of Cambridge University, on a walking tour much like those Jack took with his friends (minus the abduction and transportation to Mars); John's peregrinations, in *The Pilgrim's Regress*, are a spiritual walking tour embedded in the allegorical form. It is this connectedness with the landscape, bred from sympathetic experience, which adds an underlying spiritual dimension to the prose. The conclusion of an Irish tour with Warnie in 1933, where they sailed from Waterford, produced this exact effect when, after the first three hours out to sea, we are invited to:

Imagine a flat French grey sea, and a sky almost the same colour: between these a long fish-shaped streak of pure crimson, about 20 miles long, and lasting, unchanged or changed imperceptibly, for hours. Then add three or four perfectly *transparent* mountains, so extraordinarily spiritualised that they absolutely realised the old idea of Ireland as the 'isle of saints' ... I do not remember that I have ever seen anything more calm and spacious and celestial.[30]

There is a sensuality in Lewis's imagination that finds fruition when literature and nature meet. Whether it is the physical act of 'lying on the beach at Donaghadee reading to each other out of the Arabian Nights',[31] or lounging naked under the willows at Parsons Pleasure[32] reading George MacDonald's *Wilfred Cumbermede*, the effect is always highly charged. The attentive mind that is open to its surroundings finds unexpected delights lurking in unlikely places:

Indeed today – another of those days which I seem to have described so often lately, the same winter sunshine, the same gilt and grey skies shining thro bare shock headed bushes, the same restful pale ploughland and grass, and more than usual of the birds darting out their sudden, almost cruelly poignant songs – today I got such a sudden intense feeling of delight that it sort of stopped me in my walk and spun me round. Indeed the sweetness was so great, & seemed so to affect the whole body as well as the mind, that it gave me pause – it was so very like sex.[33]

The powerful, descriptive landscapes that we find in Jack's work stem from an imagination in tune with nature. Following a holiday at Dundrum, in the shadow of the Wicklow Mountains, Jack announces that, together with literature, 'nature … became herself the medium of the real joy'.[34] Of course neither of these could satisfy the desire, they could only serve as equal and joint reminders – act as pointers towards – God. The fusion of these disparate elements, although in Jack's case inextricably linked, came gradually together, culminating in his acceptance of Christianity.

Where we see all these aspects coming together in a coherent narrative is of course in the Narnian stories. The parallels between the Christian story and the history of Narnia are skilfully interwoven to create a story that communicates on many levels. These stories are not allegories but supposings: supposing that there was a magical world like Narnia that needed rescuing and there was only one who could? As the Son of God became a man when he came to earth, supposing that when he went to Narnia he became a lion? The writing of these stories allowed Jack to overcome a problem that had plagued him since early childhood in Belfast:

I thought I saw how stories of this kind could steal past a certain inhibition which had paralysed much of my own religion in childhood. Why did one find it so hard to feel as one was told one ought to feel about God or about the suffering of Christ? I thought the chief reason was that one was told one ought to. An obligation to feel can freeze feelings. And reverence itself did harm. The whole subject was associated with lowered voices; almost as if it were something medical. But supposing that by casting all these things into an imaginary world, stripping them of their stained-glass and Sunday school associations, one could make them for the first time appear in their real potency? Could one not thus steal past those watchful dragons? I thought one could.[35]

What matters for Lewis the author and poet is that one remains imaginatively open to the possibility of the marvellous around us. The inspiration for Narnia began with images: a picture in Jack's mind of a faun carrying an umbrella, a

The Mourne Mountains, County Down.

queen on a sledge, and a magnificent lion. For Jack, the diversity of the Irish landscape is capable of evoking similar fantastic images: 'I have seen landscapes (notably in the Mourne Mountains) which, under a particular light, made me feel that at any moment a giant might raise his head over the next ridge. Nature has that in her which compels us to invent giants: and only giants will do.'[36]

It was inevitable that Jack Lewis would feel compelled to incorporate many aspects of the Ulster countryside into his work and this is nowhere more evident than in the Narnian stories. One critic claims a direct parallel between the geography and landscapes of Narnia with those of Antrim and Down. Quoting from *The Magician's Nephew*,[37] and adding his comments in brackets, we read:

All Narnia, many-coloured with lawns and rocks and heather and different sorts of trees, lay spread out below them, the river winding through it like a ribbon of quicksilver (the Lagan). They could already see over the tops of the low hills which lay northward on their right (hills of Antrim); beyond those hills a great moorland sloped gently up and up to the horizon. On their left (southward) the mountains were much higher (Mts. of Mourne) but every now and then there was a gap when you could see, between steep pine woods, a glimpse of the southern lands that lay beyond them (now the Republic of Ireland) looking blue and far away. Their destination is the garden and magic apple tree which lie west of Narnia at the end of the blue lake (Lough Neagh) in the mountains of the Western Wild (north-western Ireland – possibly the Sperrin Mts.).[38]

This is not to say that the fictional world of Narnia is merely an imaginative representation of Ulster but rather that it is a construction: an imaginary world made out of the stuff of real life – including the author's imaginative impressions of Ireland. In reading the Narnian stories we are captivated, not solely by the environment but primarily by the tale told. For Lewis the *raison d'être* of the story is that 'we shall weep, or shudder, or wonder, or laugh as we follow it'. In attempting to trace Irish influences in the Narnian stories we should also bear in mind Jack's words on the nature of the author:

However improbable and abnormal a story he has chosen, it will, as we say, 'come to life' in his hands. The life to which it comes will be impregnated with all the wisdom, knowledge and experience the author has; and even more by something which I can only vaguely describe as the flavour or 'feel' that actual life has for him. It is this omnipresent flavour or feel that makes bad inventions so mawkish and suffocating, and good ones so tonic. The good ones allow us temporarily to share a sort of passionate sanity.[39]

The Narnian stories, as well as CS Lewis's other prose works, allow us to share in this 'passionate sanity': the religious, moral, and sociological themes in his work are all subordinated to the telling of the story and must be judged on the strength of the story itself and not the messages embedded within it.

Epilogue

Jack Lewis retained the link with his homeland throughout his life. He had been crossing the Irish sea six times a year since he was nine, during school and university holidays, and he maintained this regular contact, albeit less frequently, in his later years. Penitential visits to his father aside, Jack certainly viewed Ireland as his home while Albert was alive. Following his conversion to Christianity, shortly after his father's death, and the sale of the family home, there seems to have been a gradual shift in his perception of Ireland as 'home'. This is not to say that he did not consider himself an Irishman: as late as 1958, even after a lifetime living in England, he had no doubts as to his identity. During a recording session for a radio production due to be broadcast in America, Jack was told that his heavy breathing was playing havoc with the delicate sound recording. He replied, 'I'm Irish, not English. Did you ever know an Irishman who didn't puff and blow?'[1] Regular holidays spent with Warnie and Arthur Greeves – together with his memorable honeymoon with Joy Gresham[2] – all reinvigorated and reaffirmed his love of his homeland, albeit with certain reservations. Writing to his friend, the Catholic priest Don Giovanni Calabria, Jack notes:

… I am crossing over … to Ireland: my birthplace and dearest refuge so far as charm of landscape goes, and temperate climate, although most dreadful because of the strife, hatred and often civil war between dissenting faiths.

There indeed both yours and ours[3] 'know not by what Spirit they are led'. They take lack of charity for zeal and mutual ignorance for orthodoxy.

I think almost all the crimes which Christians have perpetrated against each other arise from this, that religion is confused with politics. For, above all other spheres of human life, the Devil claims politics for his own, as almost the citadel of his power. Let us, however, with mutual prayers pray with all our power for that charity which 'covers a multitude of sins'.[4]

This letter in many ways encapsulates Jack's feelings towards his native land; the love of the country is evident, as is his distaste for the sectarianism that afflicts it. What is clear is that after nearly half a century living on the English mainland his sense of Irishness had not been diminished.

Having been a temporary exile from Ulster since he was nine years old Jack found that the country exerted a significant influence on his imagination. It became a place linked intimately with the first sensations of Joy that he experienced as a child in Belfast. Such attachment and absorption in a place can act as a barrier to embracing new experiences, becoming merely a sort of glorified homesickness, as Jack was well aware. What really matters is that one should feel part of the land and in a letter to Arthur Greeves, Jack confides that he was now overcoming this problem and beginning to strike roots in England:

I envy you your stay at Ballycastle: even the name gives me a faint pleasant twinge. But there is one odd thing I have been noticing since we came to our new house, which is much more in the country, and it is this. Hitherto there has always been something not so much in the landscape as in every single visual impression (say a cloud, a robin, or a ditch) in Ireland, which I lacked in England: something for which homeliness is an inadequate word. This something I find I am now getting in England – the feeling of connectedness, of being part of it. I suppose I have been growing into the soil here much more since the move ... My afternoon hours of exercise have been almost wholly occupied with sawing and axing for firewood ... You have no idea what horrid work sawing is for the first week, and how delightful after that when your muscles have got used to it and your hands are hardened. Almost every afternoon as I stand at my sawing block looking as I work at the sun going down behind a line of bare pollards. Nearly always a red cannon ball sun ... I also love the sound of the saw and the flying of the sawdust ... It is absurd how remote all simple human activities have been from me all my life: so much so that when I heave up my axe I still always see myself as an illustration in Robinson Crusoe. There is something in country work of this sort that you can't get out of walks.[5]

This first taste of actual physical work was transformed by an imagination informed by literature. From his adolescence in Belfast, every meaningful thought, every sensory impression, every valuable conversation with close friends had been mediated through, or motivated by, a deeply spiritual sensibility. The creative and spiritual rebirth that occurred following his Christian conversion and the writing of *The Pilgrim's Regress* released latent sympathies and allowed him to incorporate these varieties of essentially religious experience into his life and literature. It is when God, nature, and literature meet that we catch a glimpse of the real CS Lewis:

My own eyes are not enough for me, I will see through those of others. Reality, even seen through the eyes of many is not enough. I will see what others have invented. Even the eyes of all humanity are not enough. I regret that the brutes cannot write books. Very gladly would I learn what face things present to a mouse or a bee; more gladly still would I perceive the olfactory world charged with all the information and emotion it carries for a dog … in reading great literature I become a thousand men and remain myself. Like the night sky in the Greek poem, I see with a myriad eyes, but it is still I who see. Here, as in worship, in love, in moral action, and in knowing, I transcend myself; and am never more myself than when I do.[6]

Notes

Notes to Chapter 1

1. Jonathan Bardon, *Belfast: An Illustrated History*, (Blackstaff Press, 1990), p 156.
2. Jonathan Bardon, *A History of Ulster*, (Blackstaff Press, 1997), p 394.
3. CS Lewis, *Surprised by Joy: The Shape of My Early Life*, (Fount, 1977), p 15.
4. Joe Devlin was the Nationalist MP for West Belfast (formerly MP for North Kilkenny 1902–6) from 1906 until his death in 1934. He was originally a barman and later chairman of the *Irish News*.
5. *The Lewis Papers: Memoirs of the Lewis Family, 1850–1930*, (Leeborough Press), vol. 6, p 202. Warnie edited, arranged and typed the vast pile of letters and papers inherited by his father.
6. See his son's reference to these wealthy neighbours in the unfinished 'Ulster novel', in Chapter 4 of this study.
7. Information gained from the Belfast Titanic Society.
8. CS Lewis, *Of This and Other Worlds*, Walter Hooper (ed), (Collins, 1982), in the essay, 'On Stories', p 29.
9. Sybil Gribbon, *Edwardian Belfast: A Social Profile*, (Appletree Press, 1982), pp 13–14.
10. The Sir James Corry whom Albert supported was James Porter Corry, first baronet of the name and head of the firm of James P Corry and company, shipowners, of Belfast and London, whose *Star of Erin* and *Star of Australia*, were well known at the time. Albert had apparently made a considerable impact as a political speaker for he was to be found a year later speaking on behalf of various Conservative candidates such as Mr Ewart, of William E Ewart and Company, spinning mill owners; the Rt Hon Arthur William Hill; and Gustav Wolff, Director of the Belfast Ropeworks and the Union Castle Line, who later, in conjunction with Sir Edward Harland, founded Harland & Wolff. Two letters from Sir Uchter John Mark Knox, 5th Earl of Ranfurly, (later a lord in waiting to Queen Victoria and thereafter, Governor of New Zealand) beseeching Albert to speak at meetings at home and in England on behalf of the Conservatives, give some indication of his standing within the party.
11. See, *Belfast Newsletter*, Saturday, October 10, 1885, pp 7–8.
12. *Lewis Papers*, vol. 9, p 294.
13. Ibid, vol. 2, p 14.
14. Ibid, vol. 6, p 231. Frank Frankfort Moore, though born in Limerick, was raised and

117

educated in Belfast and worked for the *Belfast Newsletter* between 1876 and 1892 before moving to London. He was a prolific author and wrote several plays including *Oliver Goldsmith*, which played at the Gaiety Theatre in Dublin.

15. The house is referred to as Mountbracken in Lewis's autobiography, *Surprised by Joy*.
16. Ibid, p 43.
17. George Sayer, *Jack: A Life of C. S. Lewis*, (Hodder and Stoughton, 1997), p 21.
18. John H MacIlwaine had been trained by Hickson and Harland before being appointed draughtsman to John Elder & Company of Glasgow. For an account of the Belfast shipbuilding industry at this time see, Michael Moss and John R Hume, *Shipbuilders to the World: 125 Years of Harland and Wolff, Belfast, 1861–1986*, (Blackstaff Press, 1986).
19. *Lewis Papers*, vol. 2, pp 90–91.
20. This is a reference to St Multose in Kinsale, County Cork.
21. Lewis, *Surprised by Joy*, p 9.
22. Ibid, p 16.
23. Rudyard Kipling's poem, 'The Land,' refers to a 'William of Warenne.' This ancestor of CS Lewis was a Norman knight.
24. *Lewis Papers*, vol. 1, p 5.
25. Lewis, *Surprised by Joy*, p 9.
26. JA Froude, preface to *The English in Ireland in the Eighteenth Century*, (London, 1881), pp 22–4.
27. 'Memoir of CS Lewis' by Warren H Lewis, in CS Lewis, *Letters*, p 22.
28. Lewis, *Surprised by Joy*, p 18.
29. Douglas Gilbert and Clyde S Kilby (eds), *C. S. Lewis: Images of his World*, (Hodder and Stoughton, 1973), p 102.
30. *Lewis Papers*, vol. 3, p 91.
31. Lewis, *Surprised by Joy*, p 18.
32. CS Lewis, *The Pilgrim's Regress*, (Fount, 1978), pp 17–18.
33. *Lewis Papers*, vol. 3, p 175.
34. Lewis, *Surprised by Joy*, p 63.
35. Ibid, p 175.
36. Ibid, p 62.
37. 'Memoir of C. S. Lewis' by Warren H Lewis in, CS Lewis, *Letters*, p 26.
38. Roger Lancelyn Green and Walter Hooper, *C. S. Lewis: A Biography*, (Souvenir Press, 1988), p 17.
39. *Lewis Papers*, vol. 2, p 112.
40. Ibid, pp 112–13.
41. Ibid, p 112.
42. See Chapter 4 of this study.
43. Essay generously supplied by Walter Hooper to the author.
44. Bardon, *A History of Ulster*, p 387.
45. Lewis, *Surprised by Joy*, p 14.
46. Walter Hooper (ed), *They Stand Together: The Letters of C. S. Lewis to Arthur Greeves (1914–1963)*, (Collins, 1979), pp 378–9.

47. *Lewis Papers*, vol. 1, p 2. Re-reading these diaries at a later date, Warnie commented on his grandfather's intense religious bigotry with the remark, 'How I would have detested the old gentleman had I known him!', *Lewis Papers*, vol. 6, p 241.

48. Quoted in *A Personal Meeting with C. S. Lewis* by David Bleakley [single sheet text distributed by David Bleakley].

49. *Lewis Papers*, vol. 1, p 311.

50. Lewis, *Surprised by Joy*, p 10.

51. *Lewis Papers*, vol. 2, p 205.

52. *Belfast Telegraph*, Saturday, 28 September 1929.

53. *Lewis Papers*, vol. 11, p 249.

54. Lewis, *Surprised by Joy*, p 100. The church referred to here is Crescent Church Assembly, University Road, Belfast.

Notes to Chapter 2

1. Lewis, *Surprised by Joy*, p 21.

2. CS Lewis, *A Grief Observed*, (Faber and Faber, 1966), p 5.

3. CS Lewis, *An Experiment in Criticism*, (Cambridge University Press, 1961), p 79.

4. Lewis, *Surprised by Joy*, p 21.

5. Ibid, p 23.

6. *Lewis Papers*, vol. 4, p 160.

7. Ibid, vol. 3, p 199.

8. 'Memoir of C. S. Lewis' by Warren H Lewis in CS Lewis, *Letters*, p 24.

9. *Lewis Papers*, vol. 3, p 26.

10. Ibid, vol. 3, p 20. The school referred to is Armagh Royal School which has a strong Anglican connection and provided a viable Ulster alternative to the English public school system.

11. Ibid, vol. 2, p 59.

12. Ibid, vol. 3, p 66.

13. Lewis, *Surprised by Joy*, p 25.

14. 'Memoir of C. S. Lewis' by Warren H Lewis in CS Lewis, *Letters*, p 39.

15. *Lewis Papers*, vol. 3, p 194.

16. Lewis, *Surprised by Joy*, pp 32–3.

17. *Lewis Papers*, vol. 10, p 99. This was the Reverend Claude Lionel Chavasse who was curate of St Mark's Church, Dundela, from 1928 to 1931.

18. Ibid, vol. 3, p 97.

19. Ibid, vol. 3, p 146.

20. Ibid, vol. 3, p 147.

21. Ibid, vol. 3, p 170.

22. Lewis, *Surprised by Joy*, pp 46–7.

23. *Lewis Papers*, vol. 3, p 222.

24. Lewis, *Surprised by Joy,* p 52.

25. Ibid, p 53.

26. ATQ Stewart, *The Ulster Crisis: Resistance to Home Rule, 1912–1914*, (Faber and Faber, 1979), p 62.

27. *Lewis Papers*, vol. 3, pp 294–5.
28. Lewis, *Surprised by Joy*, p 62.
29. Ibid, p 59.
30. Ibid, p 60.
31. Ibid, p 92.
32. Ibid, p 97.
33. *Lewis Papers*, vol. 11, pp 254–5.
34. Ibid, vol. 11, p 253.
35. Clyde S Kilby and Marjorie Lamp Mead, (eds), *Brothers and Friends: The Diaries of Major Warren Hamilton Lewis* (Harper and Row, 1982), p 278.
36. Frank Frankfort Moore, *The Ulsterman: A Story of Today*, (Hutchinson, 1914), quoted in *Brothers and Friends*, p 278.
37. *Lewis Papers*, vol. 4, p 263.
38. Ibid, p 130. Warnie adds, 'The last line would appear to set at rest for ever the vexed question as to the respective preference of Sheikhs and Caliphs. Evidently the Caliph is quite an inferior chap.'
39. Bill's father was William Hugh Patterson (1835–1918). He was educated at Royal Belfast Academical Institution. In 1851 he entered his father's ironmongery business which had offices at 13–15 Bridge Street, Belfast. He was a member of the Royal Irish Academy and the Royal Society of Antiquaries. For over fifty years he was an honorary secretary of the Belfast (now the Ulster) Society for the Prevention of Cruelty to Animals and was president of both the Belfast Natural History and Philosophical Society, and the Belfast Naturalists' Field Club. He was also a member of the board of management of both the Royal Victoria Hospital and the Belfast Government School of Art. His liberal curiosity led him to take up antiquarian researches in Ireland and he collected many artefacts, including ancient weapons and prehistoric implements. He was the author of *A Glossary of Words in Use in the Counties of Antrim and Down*, published in 1880.
40. See Chapter 1 of this study.
41. *The Lewis Papers* can be found as part of the Marion E Wade Collection at Wheaton College, Illinois.
42. *Lewis Papers*, vol. 5, p 294.
43. Ibid, p 262.

Notes to Chapter 3

1. By HMA Guerber.
2. Lewis, *Surprised by Joy*, p 106.
3. Ibid, p 109.
4. Ibid, p 113.
5. I am indebted to Walter Hooper's, *C. S. Lewis: A Companion and Guide*, (Harper Collins, 1996), pp 685–7, for this biographical information on WT Kirkpatrick.
6. Robert M Jones writing in *Royal Belfast Academical Institution Centenary Volume (1810–1910)*, (Belfast, 1913), quoted in Hooper, *C. S. Lewis: A Companion and Guide*, pp 685–6.

7. Hooper, *They Stand Together*, p 49.
8. Lewis, *Surprised by Joy*, pp 115–16.
9. Either Harland & Wolff Shipyard or Workman Clark & Company shipyard was known affectionately (though inappropriately, due to the levels of production) as 'the wee yard'. Both were close to his home.
10. Hooper, *They Stand Together*, pp 67–8.
11. CS Lewis, *Poems*, (Fount, 1994), p 171.
12. *Lewis Papers*, vol. 4, p 243.
13. These are, *The Splendid Century: Some Aspects of French Life in the Reign of Louis XIV* (1953); The *Sunset of the Splendid Century: The Life and Times of Louis Auguste de Bourbon, Duc de Maine, 1670–1736* (1955); *Assault on Olympus: The Rise of the House of Gramont between 1604 and 1678* (1958); *Louis XIV: An Informal Portrait* (1959); *The Scandalous Regent: A Life of Philippe, Duc D'Orleans, 1674–1723* (1961); *Levantine Adventurer: The Travels and Missions of the Chevalier d'Arvieux, 1653–1697* (1962); and *Memoirs of the Duc de Saint-Simon* (1964).
14. Hooper, *C. S. Lewis: A Companion and Guide*, p 700.
15. Ibid, p 700.
16. Hooper, *They Stand Together*, p 349.
17. Ibid, p 60.
18. Lewis, *Surprised by Joy*, p 127.
19. Hooper, *They Stand Together*, pp 25–6.
20. Bardon, *A History of Ulster*, p 451.
21. *Lewis Papers*, vol. 4, p 259.
22. Lewis, *Poems*, pp 229–30.
23. Hooper, *They Stand Together*, p 148.
24. Warnie had written to his father of his eagerness 'to kill some Germans' adding that should he be wounded, or worse, his name might be enrolled in 'the gleam of yonder brass' in Malvern College Chapel. *Lewis Papers*, vol. 4, pp 156–8.
25. Ibid, vol. 5, pp 228–9.
26. Hooper, *They Stand Together*, p 190.
27. Lewis, *Letters*, p 64.
28. Hooper, *They Stand Together*, p 200.
29. Colonel James Craig received his knighthood in that year and went on to become the first prime minister of Northern Ireland.
30. *Lewis Papers*, vol. 5, pp 247–8.
31. Ibid, vol. 5, pp 290–1.
32. Hooper, *They Stand Together*, p 205.
33. Ibid, p 206.
34. Lewis, *Letters*, p 84.
35. Ibid, p 87. 'Mrs Harris' was the mythical friend of Mrs Gamp in Charles Dickens's *Martin Chuzzlewit*.
36. Ibid, p 91.
37. Sayer, *Jack*, p 135.
38. The code of conduct for undergraduates was much stricter then and Jack could very well have been 'sent down' had this affair come to light.

39. The name was chosen as being, 'a complete disguise to outsiders, transparent to 'our ain folk', and will be a name which we have the best of reasons to love and honour.' Lewis, *Letters*, p 93.
40. Hooper, *They Stand Together*, p 230.
41. Lewis, *Letters*, p 103.
42. *Lewis Papers*, vol. 6, p 98.
43. Lewis, *Letters*, p 391.
44. Hooper, *They Stand Together*, p 192.
45. CS Lewis, *Poems*, p 171.

Notes to Chapter 4

1. Lewis, *Letters*, p 179.
2. Hooper, *They Stand Together*, p 187.
3. Ibid, pp 195–6.
4. Charles Wrong, 'A Chance Meeting', in James T Como, (ed), *C. S. Lewis at the Breakfast Table and Other Reminiscences*, (Collins, 1980), p 111.
5. CS Lewis, *Compelling Reason*, (Fount, 1996), p 177.
6. Lewis, *An Experiment in Criticism*, p 127.
7. Walter Hooper, (ed), *All My Road Before Me: The Diary of C. S. Lewis 1922–1927*, (Fount, 1993), p 105.
8. Hooper, *They Stand Together*, pp 470–1.
9. Ibid, p 195.
10. Ibid, p 252.
11. Arthur's homosexuality.
12. Hooper, *They Stand Together*, p 229.
13. Ibid, p 196.
14. William Force Stead (1884–1967) was born in Washington, DC, and attended the University of Virginia before he came to England. He was ordained a priest in the Church of England in 1917, graduated from Queen's College, Oxford, in 1925, and was Chaplain of Worcester College from 1927 to 1933. He was something of a poet and besides publishing his own work he had the distinction of baptising his friend and fellow poet, TS Eliot, in 1927.
15. 4 Broad Street.
16. Hooper, *They Stand Together*, p 263.
17. The visits occurred on 14 and 21 March 1921, a more detailed account of which is found in Lewis's serial letter to Warren written on the days Lewis saw Yeats (see *Letters*, pp 56–8).
18. Lewis, *Letters*, p 123.
19. Hooper, *They Stand Together*, pp 286–7.
20. Lewis, *Surprised by Joy*, p 142.
21. Hooper, *They Stand Together*, p 287.
22. From, 'Portrait of W. B. Yeats' by St John Ervine, *The Listener*, 1 September 1955, pp 331–2.
23. *The Listener*, 15 September 1955, p 427.

24. Dr John Hawkins Askins (1877–1923) was educated at Trinity College, Dublin, where he obtained a Bachelor of Medicine in 1904. He became a lieutenant in the Royal Army Medical Corps, and was promoted to captain in 1916 before being wounded in January 1917.

25. Hooper, *All My Road Before Me*, p 181.

26. Ibid, p 191.

27. Dr Robert Arthur Askins (1880–1935). Educated at Trinity College, Dublin, Bachelor of Medicine in 1907 and MD in 1913. He was commissioned a lieutenant in the Royal Army Medical Corps in 1915, a captain in 1916, and was mentioned in Despatches in August 1919. He practised medicine in Bristol for many years where he became a government medical officer. He later moved to Southern Rhodesia, where he was Director of Medical Services. In 1931 he married Mollie Whaddon, and he died at sea on 1 September 1935. They were survived by a son, Michael.

28. William James Askins (1879–1955). Educated at Trinity College, Dublin, he graduated with a BA in 1901 and became a clergyman in the Church of Ireland in 1903. He was a Curate of Kilmore Cathedral, County Cavan, 1902–6, Rector of Kilmore, 1906–30 and Dean of Kilmore Cathedral, 1931–55. He was married to Elizabeth Askins (died 1941) and later remarried. He had three children in all, Charles, Ruth, and Francis.

29. The actual cause of John Askins's illness was in dispute. The Doc believed that it was syphilis, contracted during his college days, that had doomed him to lunacy and death. However, he also claimed during this period that he had 'abandoned' a girl from Philadelphia whom he had left pregnant but later confessed she was 'a common prostitute' so the reasons for the insanity remain vague. Jack Lewis was in no doubt that the problem arose from an abnormal interest in the supernatural and the eccentric (see his letter to Arthur).

30. Hooper, *They Stand Together*, pp 292–3.

31. Ibid, pp 155–7.

32. This unfinished fragment, of over 5,300 words, was written sometime between 1924 and 1927 and represents Lewis's only attempt at a 'modern' novel. It can be found in the *Lewis Papers*, vol. 9, pp 291–300.

33. Hooper, *They Stand Together*, p 324. The quotation is a conflation of the lines 228–9 and lines 236–7 from Shakespeare's *Henry IV*, III, ii.

34. *Lewis Papers*, vol. 9, p 293.

35. See the 'Mappa Mundi' at the beginning of *The Pilgrim's Regress* for the inclusion of Wanhope as 'the Isle of Despair.'

36. Lewis, *Letters*, p 112.

37. This passage reflects Florence Lewis's own concerns about where to school her children. Writing to Albert on considering a suitable school for Warren she notes, 'there is much to be said in favour of England; would Armagh be any better than Belfast as regards accent? I doubt it'. *Lewis Papers*, vol. 3, p 20.

38. Sybil Gribbon, *Edwardian Belfast: A Social Profile*, (Appletree Press, 1982), pp 23–6.

39. Hooper, *All My Road Before Me*, p 221.

40. Hooper, *They Stand Together*, p 62.

41. Lewis, *Surprised by Joy*, p 163.
42. Lewis, *Poems*, pp 199–200.

Notes to Chapter 5

1. Hooper, *All My Road Before Me*, p 246.
2. John Norman Bryson (1896–1976) was born in Portadown, County Armagh, and educated at Queen's University, Belfast, and Merton College, Oxford. He was well known to both Jack Lewis and Arthur Greeves in later years and appears to have been well liked by those that knew him even though, as Jack noted, 'many laugh at his foppery and grumble at his laziness'. Bryson later went on to become lecturer at Balliol, Merton, and Oriel Colleges and thereafter a Fellow and Tutor in English Literature at his old college, Balliol, from 1940 to 1963.
3. Stewart, *The Ulster Crisis*, p 135.
4. *Lewis Papers*, vol. 8, p 290.
5. Lewis, *Letters*, pp 212–13.
6. Ibid, p 213.
7. CS Lewis, *Narrative Poems*, (Fount, 1994), quoted by the author in the preface to the 1950 edition, p 3.
8. WB Yeats, 'The Stares Nest by my Window', *Selected Poetry*, A Norman Jeffares, (ed), (Pan, 1974) p 118.
9. Lewis, *Narrative Poems*, p 4, preface by the author to the 1950 edition of *Dymer*.
10. Ibid, pp 54–5.
11. Ibid, p 5.
12. Ibid, preface by the author to the 1950 edition of *Dymer*, p 6.
13. Ibid, p 5.
14. Ibid, Canto VII, v. 6, 8, 9, pp 64–5.
15. Ibid, preface by the author to the 1950 edition of *Dymer*, p 5.
16. Ibid, Canto VI, v. 2.
17. Hooper, *All My Road Before Me*, pp 431–2.
18. Ibid, p 432.
19. Dr Joseph Lewis was the son of Albert's eldest brother, Joseph (1856–1908), and worked as a bacteriologist in the Belfast Infirmary in 1928. He later went on to become one of the leading haematologists in Northern Ireland.
20. Lewis, *Letters*, pp 273–4.
21. Cromlyn writing in the *Church of Ireland Gazette*, 5 February 1999.
22. Conversation with Mrs Dorothy Hill.
23. At this time, this was one of the largest department stores in Belfast, situated at Royal Avenue, not far from Albert Lewis's offices.
24. Lewis, *Letters*, pp 276–7.
25. Ibid, p 279.
26. Lewis, *Poems*, p 245.
27. Nevill Henry Kendal Almayer Coghill (1899–1980) descended from Anglo-Irish Protestant gentry and was born on 19 April 1899 at Castle Townshend, Skibbereen, County Cork. His parents were Sir Egerton Bushe Coghill, fifth baronet, a respected amateur landscape painter, and Elizabeth Hildegarde Augusta Somerville (sister of the

writer Edith Somerville). He read History and then English at Exeter College, Oxford and gained, along with CS Lewis, a first in English in 1923. He was elected Fellow of Exeter College the following year. In 1957 he was elected the Merton Professor of English Literature at Oxford. He is best known for his translation of the *Canterbury Tales* into modern English. He produced many plays for Oxford University Dramatic Society. In 1966 Coghill directed his close friend and former pupil, Richard Burton, together with Elizabeth Taylor, in *Dr Faustus* at the Oxford Playhouse.

28. Lewis, *Surprised by Joy*, p 20.
29. This is the date given in Hooper's *C. S. Lewis: A Companion and Guide*, p 577. However, in Lewis, *Poems*, pp 243–4, the date of composition is given as 1924.
30. Lewis, *Poems*, p 243.
31. See Sir James George Frazer's *The Golden Bough* (1890).
32. Lewis, *Surprised by Joy*, pp 178–9.
33. Harry Bracken, 'George Berkeley, The Irish Cartesian', in Richard Kearny (ed), *The Irish Mind: Exploring Intellectual Traditions*, (Wolfhound Press, 1985), p 113.
34. Lewis, *Surprised by Joy*, p 178.
35. Hooper, *They Stand Together*, p 425.
36. The literary discussion group that met at the Bird and Baby pub in Oxford and Jack's rooms in Magdalen College to read aloud from their work. For a full account of the group see Humphrey Carpenter's, *The Inklings*, (Harper Collins, 1997).
37. GB Tennyson, 'On Location, Without Tears', in *The California Political Review*, vol. 5, No 1 (Winter 1994), quoted in Hooper, *C. S. Lewis: A Companion and Guide*, pp 765–6.
38. 'Nine nights I hung upon the Tree, wounded with the spear as an offering to Odin, myself sacrificed to myself.'
39. Hooper, *They Stand Together*, pp 427–8.
40. Lewis, *Surprised by Joy*, p 189.
41. Ibid, p 189.
42. In hand she boldly took
    To make another like the former dame,
    Another Florimell in shape and look
    So lively and so like that many it mistook. (Spencer)
43. Lewis, *Poems*, p 213.
44. CS Lewis, *The Pilgrim's Regress*, 3rd edn, p 10.
45. Ibid, p 15.
46. Ibid, p 33.
47. Ibid, p 20.
48. Ibid, p 247.
49. *Lewis Papers*, vol. 11, p 253.
50. Carpenter, *The Inklings*, p 50.
51. CS Lewis, *Mere Christianity*, (Fontana, 1975), p 7.
52. Hooper, *They Stand Together*, pp 474–5.
53. Ibid, p 452.
54. Lewis, *The Pilgrim's Regress*, p 249.
55. Ibid, p 250.

Notes to Chapter 6

1. Hooper, *All My Road Before Me*, p 189.
2. Ibid, pp 190–1.
3. Lewis, *Surprised by Joy*, p 170.
4. John Betjeman was reading English Literature at Magdalen College, Oxford. He matriculated in 1924 but went down from Oxford without a degree. He later succeeded Cecil Day-Lewis (who had defeated CS Lewis for the Chair of Poetry at Oxford in 1951 by a slim majority of 21 votes) as Poet Laureate in 1972.
5. Hooper, *All My Road Before Me*, pp 413–4.
6. Humphrey Carpenter, *The Inklings*, (George Allen and Unwin, 1978), p 49.
7. Lewis, *Poems*, p 15.
8. Letter from Nevill Coghill to Clyde S Kilby in the essay 'The Creative Logician Speaking' in Carolyn Keefe (ed), *C. S. Lewis: Speaker and Teacher*, (Hodder and Stoughton, 1971), pp 21–2.
9. Kilby and Lamp Mead, *Brothers and Friends*, p 197.
10. Amanda McKittrick Ros, *Irene Iddesleigh*, (Boni and Liveright, 1927).
11. On the day CS Lewis died, Friday, 22 November 1963, John F Kennedy was assassinated in Dallas, Texas and another author and admirer of Amanda McKittrick Ros, Aldous Huxley, departed this world, under spectacular LSD-induced visions, in California.
12. *Lewis Papers*, vol. 4, p 294.
13. This letter was written on 8 December 1905 to Albert Lewis and was sent by Warnie Lewis to the author, Jack Loudan. See, Jack Loudan, *O Rare Amanda: The Life of Amanda McKittrick Ros,* (Chatto and Windus, 1954), p 99.
14. Hooper, *All My Road Before Me*, p 437.
15. Michael Longley (ed), *Louis MacNeice, Selected Poems*, (Faber and Faber, 1988), p 15.
16. Clyde S Kilby (ed), *C. S. Lewis: Letters to an American Lady*, (Hodder and Stoughton, 1969), p 34.
17. Hooper, *They Stand Together*, p 380.
18. 'Notes on the Way', *Time and Tide*, vol. 27, June 1946, pp 510–1.
19. Hooper, *They Stand Together*, p 509.
20. Hooper, *All My Road Before Me*, p 127.
21. Ibid, p 131.
22. *The Irish Citizen*, 25 July 1914.
23. Hooper, *All My Road Before Me*, pp 127–8.
24. Ibid, p 154.
25. Lewis, *Surprised by Joy*, p 124.
26. Ibid, pp 124–6.
27. Hooper, *They Stand Together*, p 324.
28. Ibid, p 322.
29. Ibid, pp 341–2.
30. Ibid, p 458.
31. Ibid, p 406.

32. The nude bathing place for male undergraduates on the River Cherwell, just north of Magdalen College, Oxford.
33. Hooper, *They Stand Together*, p 338. Lewis goes on to add, 'One knows what a psychoanalyst would say – it is sublimated lust, a kind of defecated masturbation which fancy gives one to compensate for external chastity. Yet after all, why should that be the right way of looking at it? If he can say that "It" is sublimated sex, why is it not open to me to say that sex is undeveloped "It"? – as Plato would have said.'
34. Lewis, *Surprised by Joy*, p 66.
35. Hooper, *CS Lewis, Of This and Other Worlds*, in the essay, 'Sometimes Fairy Stories May Say Best What's To Be Said', p 73.
36. Ibid, in the essay, 'On Stories', p 31.
37. CS Lewis, *The Magician's Nephew*, (Lions, 1987), p 136.
38. Professor FS Kastor, 'C. S. Lewis and Holy Ireland' in *Search* (vol. 21, No 1, Spring 1998), p 179.
39. Lewis, *An Experiment in Criticism*, pp 81–2.

Notes to Epilogue

1. Keefe, *C. S. Lewis: Speaker and Teacher*, p 166.
2. Joy Davidman Gresham was an American correspondent of CS Lewis. She first met Jack in 1952 and the two were married in a civil ceremony in 1956 (a marriage conducted to enable Joy to claim British citizenship) and shortly afterwards she discovered that she had cancer. On 21 March 1957 she and Lewis were married by a Church of England clergyman at her bedside in the Wingfield-Morris Hospital, Oxford. Following a brief remission from the cancer the couple took a belated honeymoon in Ireland in 1958. Joy died on 13 July 1960.
3. Catholic and Protestant.
4. Martin Moynihan (ed), *Letters, C. S. Lewis / Don Giovanni Calabria: A Study in Friendship*, (Collins, 1989), p 83. This correspondence, conducted in Latin, took place between Don Giovanni Calabria (now the Blessed Giovanni Calabria – his beatification took place in Verona in 1988) and CS Lewis from 1947 until Calabria's death in 1954.
5. Hooper, *They Stand Together*, p 397.
6. Lewis, *An Experiment in Criticism*, pp 140–1.

Bibliography

Jonathan Bardon, *Belfast: An Illustrated History*, (Blackstaff, 1990).

Jonathan Bardon, *A History of Ulster*, (Blackstaff, 1997).

Humphrey Carpenter, *The Inklings*, (Harper Collins, 1997).

James T Como (ed), *C. S. Lewis at the Breakfast Table and Other Reminiscences*, (Collins, 1980).

Sybil Gribbon, *Edwardian Belfast: A Social Profile*, (Appletree Press, 1982).

George Sayer, *Jack*, (Hodder and Stoughton, 1997).

JA Froude, *The English in Ireland in the Eighteenth Century*, (London, 1881).

'Memoir of C. S. Lewis' by Warren H Lewis, *Letters*, (Fount, 1988).

Douglas Gilbert and Clyde S Kilby (eds), *C. S. Lewis: Images of his World*, (Hodder and Stoughton, 1973).

Roger Lancelyn Green and Walter Hooper, *C. S. Lewis: A Biography*, (Souvenir Press, 1988).

Walter Hooper (ed), *They Stand Together: The Letters of C. S. Lewis to Arthur Greeves (1914–1963)*, (Collins, 1979).

Walter Hooper (ed), *All My Road Before Me: The Diary of C. S. Lewis 1922–1927*, (Fount, 1993).

Walter Hooper, *C. S. Lewis: A Companion and Guide*, (Harper Collins, 1996).

A Norman Jeffares (ed), *W. B. Yeats, Selected Poetry*, (Pan, 1974).

Richard Kearny (ed), *The Irish Mind: Exploring Intellectual Traditions*, (Wolfhound Press, 1985).

Carolyn Keefe (ed), *C. S. Lewis: Speaker and Teacher*, (Hodder and Stoughton, 1971).

Clyde S Kilby (ed), *C. S. Lewis: Letters to an American Lady*, (Hodder and Stoughton, 1969).

Clyde S Kilby and Marjorie Lamp Mead (eds), *Brothers and Friends: The Diaries of Major Warren Hamilton Lewis*, (Harper and Row, 1982).

CS Lewis, *An Experiment in Criticism*, (Cambridge University Press, 1961).

CS Lewis, *A Grief Observed*, (Faber and Faber, 1966).

CS Lewis, *Mere Christianity*, (Fontana, 1975).

CS Lewis, *Surprised by Joy*, (Fount, 1977).

CS Lewis, *Of This and Other Worlds* (Walter Hooper, ed), (Collins, 1982).

CS Lewis, *The Magician's Nephew*, (Lions, 1987).

CS Lewis, *Narrative Poems*, (Fount, 1994).

CS Lewis, *Poems*, (Fount, 1994).

CS Lewis, *Compelling Reason*, (Fount, 1996).

Michael Longley (ed), Louis MacNeice, *Selected Poems*, (Faber and Faber, 1988).

Jack Loudan, *O Rare Amanda: The Life of Amanda McKittrick Ros,* (Chatto and Windus, 1954).

Amanda McKittrick Ros, *Irene Iddesleigh*, (New York: Boni and Liveright, 1927).

Frank Frankfort Moore, *The Ulsterman: A Story of Today*, (Hutchinson, 1914).

Martin Moynihan (ed), *Letters, C. S. Lewis / Don Giovanni Calabria: A Study in Friendship*, (Collins, 1989).

ATQ Stewart, *The Ulster Crisis: Resistance to Home Rule, 1912–1914*, (Faber and Faber, 1979).

William Mullan & Sons Ltd children's bookshop in Fountain Street, Belfast, 1937 show-ing the enthusiasm for reading in CS Lewis's home city.

Select list of works by CS Lewis

Poetry

1919 *Spirits in Bondage: A Cycle of Lyrics*
1926 *Dymer*
1964 *Poems*, (edited by Walter Hooper)
1969 *Narrative Poems*, (edited by Walter Hooper)

Children's books

1950 *The Lion, the Witch and the Wardrobe*
1951 *Prince Caspian*
1952 *The Voyage of the 'Dawn Treader'*
1953 *The Silver Chair*
1954 *The Horse and His Boy*
1955 *The Magician's Nephew*
1956 *The Last Battle*
1985 *Letters to Children*, (edited by Lyle W Dorsett and Marjorie L Mead)

Academic

1936 *The Allegory of Love: A Study in Medieval Tradition*
1942 *A Preface to Paradise Lost*
1948 *Arthurian Torso*
1954 *English Literature in the 16th Century Excluding Drama.* Vol. 3 of *The Oxford History of English Literature*
1960 *Studies in Words*
1961 *An Experiment in Criticism*
1964 *The Discarded Image: An Introduction to Medieval and Renaissance Literature*

Autobiography

1955 *Surprised by Joy: The Shape of My Early Life*
1961 *A Grief Observed*

Christian writings

1933 *The Pilgrim's Regress*
1940 *The Problem of Pain*
1942 *The Screwtape Letters*
1946 *The Great Divorce*
1947 *Miracles*
1949 *The Weight of Glory*
1952 *Mere Christianity*
1958 *Reflections on the Psalms*
1960 *The Four Loves*
1964 *Letters to Malcolm: Chiefly on Prayer*

Science fiction/fantasy

1938 *Out of the Silent Planet*
1943 *Perelandra*
1945 *That Hideous Strength*
1977 *The Dark Tower & Other Stories*, (edited by Walter Hooper)

Novels

1956 *Till We Have Faces*

Letters and diaries

1966 *Letters of C.S. Lewis*, (edited by Warren H Lewis)
1967 *Letters to an American Lady*, (edited by Clyde Kilby)
1979 *They Stand Together: Letters to Arthur Greeves*, (edited by Walter Hooper)
1989 *Letters, C. S. Lewis/Don Giovanni Calabria: A Study in Friendship*, (edited by Martin Moynihan)
1991 *All My Road Before Me: The Diary of C. S. Lewis 1922–1927*, (edited by Walter Hooper)

Acknowledgement of sources

Permission to use extracts from published and unpublished material has been granted by the following publishers and bodies.

The Institute of Irish Studies has made every effort to trace the copyright-holders of the work in this book. If there are any omissions the Institute of Irish Studies will happily correct this in reprints or future editions of the book. Copyright is unaltered by publication in this book.

All My Road Before Me by CS Lewis © 1991; *Boxen* by CS Lewis © 1985; *Companion and Guide* by CS Lewis © 1996; *Compelling Reason* by CS Lewis ©1996; *Letters of CS Lewis* by CS Lewis © 1996; *The Lewis Papers, Memoirs of the Lewis Family*, extracts by CS Lewis ©; *The Magician's Nephew* by CS Lewis © 1955; *Mere Christianity* by CS Lewis © 1942, 1943, 1944, 1952; *Narrative Poems* by CS Lewis © 1969; *Of This and Other Worlds* by CS Lewis © 1966; *The Pilgrim's Regress* by CS Lewis © 1933; *Poems* by CS Lewis © 1964; *Surprised by Joy* by CS Lewis © 1955; and *They Stand Together* by CS Lewis © 1979: all copyright C.S. Lewis Pte Ltd, extracts reprinted by permission.

The Lewis Papers, extracts by Flora and Albert Lewis copyright © C.S. Lewis Pte Ltd and the Marion E. Wade Center, Wheaton College, Illinois USA, 1999.

American editions: excerpts from *All My Road Before Me: The Diary of C. S. Lewis 1922–1927* by CS Lewis, copyright © 1991 by C.S. Lewis Pte Ltd; excerpts from *Letters of C. S. Lewis* by CS Lewis, copyright © 1966 by W.H. Lewis and the Executors of the Estate of C.S. Lewis and renewed 1994 by C.S. Lewis Pte Ltd; excerpts from *Narrative Poems* by CS Lewis, copyright © 1969 and renewed 1997 by C.S. Lewis Pte Ltd, preface copyright © 1969 by Walter Hooper; excerpts from *Of Other Worlds: Essays and Stories* by CS Lewis, copyright © 1966 by the Executors of the Estate of C.S. Lewis and renewed 1994 by C.S. Lewis Pte Ltd; excerpts from *Poems* by CS Lewis, copyright © 1964 by the Executors of the Estate of C.S. Lewis and renewed 1992 by C.S. Lewis Pte Ltd; and excerpts from *Surprised by Joy: The Shape of My Early Life* by CS Lewis, copyright © 1956 by C.S. Lewis Pte Ltd, and renewed 1984 by Arthur Owen Barfield: all reprinted by permission of Harcourt, Inc.

Brothers and Friends: The Diaries of Major Warren Hamilton Lewis, copyright the Marion E. Wade Center, Wheaton College, Illinois USA, 1982.

Collected Poems by Louis MacNeice reproduced by kind permission of Faber.

CS Lewis, Letters to an American Lady, edited by Clyde S Kilby,©1967 by Wm B Eerdmans Publishing Company, Grand Rapids, Michigan. Reprinted by permission of the publisher; all rights reserved.

Illustrations

Index